The book introduces zemiology as a discip
language' of conventional criminology and n
concern of all scholar-activists. Zemiology a
that lots of harms around the world are leg
clude that the pursuit of corporate profits at the expense of human needs is the main driver of social harms. They call for the abolition of capitalism as part of efforts towards harm-reduction.

Biko Agozino, *Professor of Sociology and Africana Studies, Virginia Tech*

This book is timely and provides an easily accessible, theoretical and empirical introduction to zemiology, the discipline that seeks to unearth harmful structures, policies, decisions and practice to generate changes to confront them. After a pedagogical introduction covering the arguments in favour of zemiology as a discipline of its own, the book unpacks theoretical and empirical demonstrations that clearly underline the field's justification. As the authors state, *zemiology requires a rethink about the lens through which we view the world in which we live.* This is an important book for students and others who want to look beyond criminology to understand, analyse and act against harms.

Ragnhild Sollund, *Professor of Criminology at the University of Oslo*

FROM SOCIAL HARM TO ZEMIOLOGY

This book outlines key developments in understanding social harm by setting out its historical foundations and the discussions which have proliferated since. It examines various attempts to conceptualise social harm and highlights key sites of contestation in its relationship to criminology to argue that these act as the basis for an activist zemiology, one directed towards social change for social justice. The past two decades have seen a proliferation of debate related to social harm in and around criminology. From climate catastrophe and a focus on environmental harms, unprecedented deaths generating focus on border harms and the coronavirus pandemic revealing the horror of mass and arguably avoidable deaths across the globe, critical studies in social harm appear ever more pressing.

Drawing on a range of international case studies of cultural, emotional, physical and economic harms, *From Social Harm to Zemiology* locates the study of social harm in an accessible fashion. In doing so it sets out how a zemiological lens can move us beyond many of the problematic legacies of criminology. This book rejects criminologies which have disproportionately served to regulate intersectional groups, and which have arguably inflicted as much or more harm by bolstering the very ideologies of control in offering minor reforms that inadvertently expand and strengthen states and corporations. It does this by sketching out the contours, objects, methods and ontologies of a disciplinary framework which rejects commonplace assumptions of 'value freedom'. *From Social Harm to Zemiology* advocates social change in accordance with groups who are most disenfranchised, and thus often most socially harmed.

An accessible and compelling read, this book is essential reading for all zemiologists, critical criminologists and those engaged with criminological and social theory.

Victoria Canning is a Senior Lecturer in Criminology at the University of Bristol. She is currently co-coordinator of the European Group for the Study of Deviance and Social Control, Associate Director in Border Criminologies at Oxford University and a trustee of Statewatch. She researches violence, harm and torture, and has worked for more than a decade on migrant rights and women's rights.

Steve Tombs is Professor of Criminology at The Open University. He has a long-standing interest in the incidence, nature and regulation of corporate and state crime and harm. He has long worked with the Hazards movement in the UK, and is a trustee and board member of Inquest.

New Directions in Critical Criminology

This series presents new cutting-edge critical criminological empirical, theoretical, and policy work on a broad range of social problems, including drug policy, rural crime and social control, policing and the media, ecocide, intersectionality, and the gendered nature of crime. It aims to highlight the most up-to-date authoritative essays written by new and established scholars in the field. Rather than offering a survey of the literature, each book takes a strong position on topics of major concern to those interested in seeking new ways of thinking critically about crime.

Edited by Walter S. DeKeseredy, West Virginia University, USA

Intersectionality and Criminology
Disrupting and Revolutionizing Studies of Crime
Hillary Potter

Queer Criminology
Carrie L. Buist and Emily Lenning

Crime, Justice and Social Media
Michael Salter

Southern Criminology
Kerry Carrington, Russell Hogg, John Scott, Máximo Sozzo and Reece Walters

Sex-Positive Criminology
Aimee Wodda and Vanessa R. Panfil

Social Democratic Criminology
Robert Reiner

From Social Harm to Zemiology
A Critical Introduction
Victoria Canning and Steve Tombs

For more information about this series, please visit: https://www.routledge.com/New-Directions-in-Critical-Criminology/book-series/NDCC

FROM SOCIAL HARM TO ZEMIOLOGY

A Critical Introduction

Victoria Canning and Steve Tombs

LONDON AND NEW YORK

First published 2021
by Routledge
2 Park Square, Milton Park, Abingdon, Oxon OX14 4RN

and by Routledge
52 Vanderbilt Avenue, New York, NY 10017

Routledge is an imprint of the Taylor & Francis Group, an informa business

British Library Cataloguing-in-Publication Data
A catalogue record for this book is available from the British Library

Library of Congress Cataloging-in-Publication Data
A catalog record has been requested for this book

ISBN: 978-1-138-36608-4 (hbk)
ISBN: 978-1-138-36609-1 (pbk)
ISBN: 978-0-429-43049-7 (ebk)

Typeset in Bembo
by Newgen Publishing UK

CONTENTS

FIGURES

TABLES

BOXES

PREFACE

It is a pleasure to be asked to write a preface for the first student text on zemiology. It is now well over 20 years since a number of my colleagues and I began to think about the development of a new discipline dedicated to the study of all aspects of social harm which people experience from the cradle to the grave. While recognising the progressive developments in critical criminology, we considered that the limitations of criminology – in particular, its straight jacket of state-defined crime and the need to study key modules on crime, policing, criminal 'justice' and prisons – made it difficult to move beyond the criminological gaze and develop new thinking both at the theoretical and policy level. We therefore proposed the establishment of a separate discipline which would study of the whole range of social harms, not just those defined by the state as criminal.

The Covid-19 pandemic is causing an unprecedented amount of physical, financial, social and cultural harm throughout the world highlighting starkly the vast inequalities which exist globally and within states. In the United Kingdom alone the virus killed more people in the first 65 days than all the homicides recorded in England, Wales, Scotland and Northern Ireland in the 38 years from 1980 to 2018. Yet we had been warned about the possibility of a pandemic. In 2005 Mike Davis published *The Monster at Our Door* which explored the threat of a pandemic from Asian Flu exposing the central roles played by agribusiness, the food industry and the burgeoning slums, and the willingness of societies to privilege profit above public health. Even Hollywood predicted it! In 2011 Matt Damon starred in *Contagion*, directed by Steven Soderbergh, which accurately portrayed the horrifying impact of a pandemic. Yet most governments failed to plan. The continuing social harm caused by the pandemic will soon be exacerbated by the United Kingdom's withdrawal from the European Union. Overarching all these developments is climate change, which is causing a myriad of preventable social harms throughout the world and an existential threat to life on this planet. Yet governments continue to act expeditiously.

There has therefore never been a more opportune time to publish a book which expands our understanding of social harm. It begins by charting the development of thinking behind the need for a discipline of zemiology and presents some of the critiques of such a development. It identifies the varieties and characteristics of social harm, discusses the theoretical and intellectual challenges for the new discipline and it sets out some elements of and the potential for zemiological research. Typically, responses to harm focus on the individual; this is particularly true in relation to harms defined by the state. Zemiology, as this book makes clear throughout the chapters, shifts the focus to institutions, structures and ideology.

When I coined the name 'zemiology', combining the Greek word for harm, 'zemia', with 'ology', I wanted to construct a totally new word, which would have no meaning other than that developed through its usage. The aim was to develop new thinking about social harm without the baggage of meanings associated with commonly used words learnt from the moment a child learns to speak English and to challenge traditional ways of seeing, talking about, analysing and responding to social harm. As the authors emphasise 'in doing zemiology', it is important to reflect on language and how it is used and exercised. Words are not neutral, they carry power.

In a recent tweet, Mariame Kaba, an American prison abolitionist, critiqued the deliberate suffocation of people's aspirations. She complained about people who constantly: "scream about ⋆realism⋆ and try to foreclose even ⋆thinking⋆ about something else, something different than the current order". She described this suffocation poignantly as "spirit-murder".[1] This book, which is written in a clear and accessible style, provides an excellent platform for new thinking around social harm, and an antidote to spirit-murder.

Paddy Hillyard, Belfast, September 2020

Note

1 My thanks to Megan Nolan for drawing attention to the tweet. See *New Statesman*, 2–8 October 2020.

ACKNOWLEDGEMENTS

Any piece of writing is the product of a long series of experiences, relationships, encounters, debates and reflection, and this is no different.

Amongst the hundreds of academics and activists with whom we directly and indirectly have worked and the organisations with which we have most fruitfully engaged, we would especially like to thank the following: Dalia Abdelhady, Biko Agozino, Monish Bhatia, *Border Criminologies*, Avi Boukli, Tony Bunyan, *Centre for Crime, Criminalisation and Social Exclusion*, Matthew Cole, Roy Coleman, *Centre for Global Criminology at Copenhagen University*, Deborah Coles, Vicky Cooper, Lynne Copson, *Danish Institute Against Torture*, Deanna Dadusc, Eleni Dimou, Andrew Douglas, Deborah Drake, *European Group for the Study of Deviance and Social Control*, *Harm and Evidence Research Collaborative*, *Hazards*, *INQUEST*, Andrew Jefferson, Daniel Jiménez Franco, Keir Irwin-Rogers, Martin Joormann, *Lund University Department of Sociology of Law,* Lisa Matthews, Will McMahon, Dan McCulloch, *Migrant Artists Mutual Aid*, Ida Nafstad, Hilda Palmer, Christina Pantazis, Frank Pearce, Simon Pemberton, Graham Pike, Lozzie Potter, *RFSL Newcomers Malmö*, Rebecca Roberts, *Right to Remain*, David Sausdal, David Scott, Joe Sim, Katja Simončič, Alex Simpson, Ann Singleton, *Statewatch*, Henrik Vigh, Lisa White, David Whyte.

Particular thanks go to Paddy Hillyard, who has long been a friend and an inspiration and with whom we are privileged to have begun the journey towards zemiology.

Vicky wishes to thank her family, and especially Drew for all his support, in particular during the 2020 pandemic and while writing this book.

Finally, Steve wishes to thank Linda. She knows why.

INTRODUCTION

Social harm matters

In the late 1990s a group of academics and activists began a series of conversations about how a concept of social harm could be more progressively developed as an alternative to increasingly dominant notions of crime. While the motivations of, or routes via which, individuals who joined these conversations were various, these developed into the book *Beyond Criminology: Taking Harm Seriously* (Hillyard *et al.*, 2004). It was here and later (Hillyard and Tombs, 2008) that the study of zemiology began to take shape academically.

Since the publication of Hillyard *et al.*'s 2004 collection there has been a proliferation of debate related to social harm. Historically, much of this has been based in criminology, but as time has gone by other disciplines have developed to encompass – and be encompassed by – studies in social harm. Deteriorations in the environment with the exacerbation of climate catastrophe and global warming have facilitated insight into environmental harms. Unprecedented deaths at global borders remind us that those who are most harmed by bordering are often those who are in most need of having access to mobility, and thus studies in social harms align with human geography. The catastrophic and ongoing harms inflicted by the foreseen economic crisis of 2007/2008 combine critical studies in economics with studies in social harm. Indeed, when we unpack powerful structures and institutions to consider who they serve and who they disproportionately harm, we are able to move forward with a clear and specific disciplinary focus on harmful practices: zemiology. It is with zemiology, a discipline that seeks to unearth harmful structures, policies, decisions and practices, evidences the impacts that they have and thus generates sustainable and radical changes so that they may be mitigated or eradicated, which we are concerned with here.

We completed this text in the midst of a devastatingly up-close view of such state-imposed social harm. From the very end of 2019 onwards, and through 2020, Governments around the globe were all confronted with the novel, deadly challenge of coronavirus. Across the globe there were significant variations in the level of preparedness for a health pandemic and then when and how Governments approached the management of Covid-19 in particular – with markedly differing aims and, importantly, outcomes (Pearce *et al.*, 2020), with 'what works', too, varying markedly (see, for example, Ariadne Labs, 2020; Pollack *et al.*, 2020; Wieler *et al.*, 2020).

What this of course tells us is that if the virus was a naturally occurring phenomenon – viruses, after all, are essential agents of human existence (Witzany, 2012) – the disaster that it provoked was not at all natural – natural. It was social, the result of social priorities and choices, related to existing economic and social inequalities, and to decisions to maintain or develop systems of health care and social protection which were more or less robust, more or less effective, more or less harm preventing or mitigating.

One of the other conversations that emerged as the effects of the virus began to become manifest was how to measure the harms that it had produced – and would continue to produce. Most crudely, these were measured in the most extreme form of physical harm, namely loss of life (even if there were considerable controversies in determining who or what counted as a coronavirus death in many jurisdictions). But to measure the harms generated by the virus in deaths alone is wholly inadequate. Many lives have been changed detrimentally by the lasting health effects of contracting the virus. Nor is there any knowing, for example, the emotional and psychological trauma experienced during lockdowns, as a result of fear, isolation, bereavement, abuse within households and so on, nor the damage caused by the closure of schools, in some states for months, nor of the legacies of the recessions that have begun to unfold following the first wave of the virus – with the concomitant un- and under-employment, deprivation, increases in poverty-related illnesses and morbidities, suicides, and so on. Nor is it to account for the harms associated with the damages to the cultural lives of states and their citizens – theatre, film and music industries have all been altered irrevocably and detrimentally. All of these harms – and the dimensions of harm are far greater than indicated here – will continue to be felt across the globe for years to come, irrespective of how the virus is managed in national and international contexts in the future.

Do we really need another 'ology'?

During the course of writing this book, we had many discussions with – and encountered considerable scepticism from – academics and activists who asked if there was truly a need for *another* 'ology'. Even though the term *zemiology* had already been coined in the mid-1990s, for some it seemed and remains an 'ology' too far. Some scholars in criminology have already repeatedly described zemiology as a sub-discipline, sitting under the umbrella of the multi-disciplinary study of crime. However, our objective here is to separate the notion of harm as being intrinsically connected with 'crime'. Crime is a social construct, developed almost exclusively through state-centric and historically elitist approaches to the social control of deviant – and indeed sometimes harmful – practices or actions. The primary outcome has been the creation of localised and globalised modes of 'criminal' justice. With the exception of, for example, the International Criminal Courts or those laws which (almost always wholly inadequately) seek to regulate corporate activities, notions of crime continue to fixate upon low level crimes of the powerless and justify focus on individualistic forms of accountability through, for example, confinement in prisons.

This causes us concern for three main reasons.

First, by using normative language around 'crime', we inadvertently reproduce crime as a social truth, as though it is a natural rather than a social construct. We assume everyone knows what we mean by 'crime', and yet – as we highlight here – crime is both spatially and temporally contingent. It is not static, and it does not mean the same geographically or over time. This does not mean that criminology itself is not relevant to us – indeed, in particular for Steve, redefining what is meant by 'crime' has been a central facet to his work regarding corporate and white-collar crime. However, developing and adopting a social harm approach to a subject does not mean that crime and criminology are irrelevances (see Box I.1 on the Grenfell Tower fire). What it does mean is that a deeper analysis of harm in relation to many social phenomena and problems facilitates a multi-dimensional understanding in ways that a focus on crime *per se* cannot do, in the process uncovering otherwise unseen or under-recognised harms and at least creating the potential that these might be addressed.

Second, and building on this point, is our shared concern that the issues which harm us most, and from which people are most likely to be harmed, made ill or even die, are completely unconnected to crime. The ongoing global health crisis is the most stark indication of this. Instead, many of our most serious problems – malnutrition, child poverty, pollution-induced premature deaths – relate to structural or institutional violence for which it is difficult or impossible to hold individuals or organisations to account. These are based more often than not in broader policy or structures rather than 'crime'. Thus the key aim of zemiology is social justice. This requires, as Tombs and Whyte (2015) earlier argued in this Routledge book series, the abolition of corporations and a fundamental restructuring away from

BOX I.1 GRENFELL: A SITE OF CRIME AND HARM

Grenfell Tower was a high-rise block of mostly social housing flats in the Royal Borough of Kensington and Chelsea – the richest borough in London. On 14 June 2017, 72 people died as the block broke into an inferno. Through the fire we can see how the same phenomenon can usefully be viewed through the lens of crime and also social harm – with different aspects of that phenomenon thereby revealed. Through a criminological lens, the fire raises clear issues for state and corporate accountability. There was already evidence that the Grenfell Tower residents had highlighted the potential dangers of the material that became responsible for the speed of fire spreading: the cladding. For a saving of £293,368, cheaper aluminium cladding was used in refurbishments instead of the safer zinc substitute. The Grenfell Action Group had already warned of a tragedy back in 2016. The Royal Borough of Kensington and Chelsea Council ignored its warnings. It is possible that the acts and omissions which produced the fire will ultimately lead to some form of criminal prosecutions, perhaps of organisations, of individuals, or both, whether under fire or health and safety legislation or, indeed, the Corporate Manslaughter and Corporate Homicide Act.

However, whatever unfolds in terms of crime, regulation, prosecution and/or legal reform, a sole focus on law would obscure the plethora of harms inherent in the avoidable Grenfell disaster. Whilst harm is obvious in the case of 72 deaths, scraping the surface evidences many unseen harms for survivors and witnesses.

- Other physical harms took the form of life-changing injuries as well as ill-health effects as a result of exposure to airborne toxins generated by the fire, as well as through exacerbation of existing health problems.
- Surviving the fire in Grenfell Tower is most obviously likely to have produced a whole gamut of searing psychological and emotional problems with which victims and many across the local community will live for years to come – even within a month or so of the fire, reports began to circulate about suicide attempts and other manifestations of long-term mental health problems, including PTSD, stress, depression and anxiety.
- Moreover, there is no way of knowing what financial costs were, and continue to be, incurred by former residents of the Tower, as well as those living in the vicinity (but they would include extra travel

costs to work or school, the costs of eating out, of time off to attend meetings, funerals, medical appointments, and so on).
- These costs are dwarfed by those to local, regional and national economies which are likely to follow the fire.
- In terms of cultural harms, it is clear that in their physical relocation from the Tower and area – their dispersal – that many of both the routines and the networks which constitute social life – at school, the local shops, around the flats and so on – have been rent asunder.
- There were significant relational harms that followed from mistrust of central and local government, each of which were absent in the immediate aftermath of the fire, and for which PM May apologised; this mistrust was then exacerbated through a series of broken promises, half-truths and lies. In general, the residents of the tower were subject to contempt. Some recognised this contempt as a cause of the fire per se: as one resident stated outside the tower as it continued to burn, "We're dying in there because we don't count."

Source: Tombs (2019, 2020)

current socio-political modes of capitalistic means of production. Replicating reformative agendas within the same foundations is not a move which sustains the overhaul of harmful societies. In Audre Lorde's words, the master's tools will never dismantle the master's house (Lorde, 2017: 16).

Third, and finally, we acknowledge that wrongdoings which transgress laws can and do have serious impacts upon those who are subjected to them. We see the study of such interactions as a necessary and legitimate venture. Zemiology, however, lends itself to more sustained focus upon the effects of macro-level inequalities and so with patterns of harm, abuses and violences which are enacted by or as a result of those who are most powerful: states, corporations and supranational bodies. We advocate critical analyses at these levels alongside methods which generate insight into the micro-level realities of those whose lives are disproportionately lost or detrimentally affected by the impacts of such actions, decisions and omissions.

A zemiological lens thus moves us away from many toxic aspects of the histories of criminology more broadly – it is an outright rejection of dominant language which has served to control those who are most economically, politically and structurally powerless in society, specifically working classes, Black communities, women, LGBTQI people and communities, people with disabilities and those of lower caste. Going forward, we contend zemiology should separate itself from histories based in subjects which have disproportionately served to regulate these intersectional groups, and which have arguably inflicted as much or more harm by bolstering the very ideologies of control in offering minor reforms that inadvertently expand and strengthen states and corporations. It is a discipline and a framework which rejects commonplace assumptions of 'objectivity' and advocates social change in accordance with groups who are most disenfranchised, and thus often most socially harmed.

Aims and structure

This book aims to outline key developments in understanding social harm, setting out its historical foundations and the discussions which have proliferated since. It outlines various attempts to conceptualise social harm, and highlights key sites of contestation in its relationship to criminology and, then, as the basis for zemiology. The objectives of this book are five-fold:

- first, to map out the foundations of the development of zemiology, including analyses of critiques thereof;
- second, to identify the varieties and characteristics of social harm;
- third, to specify the concept of social harm, as precisely as the current state of knowledge allows, and thereby to allow it to form the basis of zemiology;
- fourth, through presenting a range of case study examples, to extend the focus of previous texts on the Global North, and to emphasise that many harms need to be understood globally;
- fifth, to set out some elements of and the potential for 'doing' zemiology – for students, academics, practitioners and activists.

As evidenced by their recent inclusion in the Quality Assurance Agency's benchmark statements for criminology, social harm and zemiology are emerging areas of study both with and beyond criminology (Quality Assurance Agency, 2014, 2019). As of yet however, there has been no definitive book written which is aimed specifically at undergraduate and postgraduate courses. We hope that this book will be accessible for those working across the social sciences, including but not restricted to sociology, social policy, criminology, human geography, politics and political economy. It is our hope, too, that what we have to say will be of use and interest to practitioners and campaigners working across an array of fields where mitigating harm is the primary focus, even if harms are not explicitly conceptualised – such as in education, housing, the criminal justice system, refugee support, welfare, health and social services, and workplaces.

Chapter 1 defines the term and usage of the word 'zemiology': its origins in the Greek *xemia*, or harm, and its use in studying *social* harm, and will briefly introduce dimensions of harm. It maps the historical use of the term as an approach to studying social problems which is alternative to – but linked with – criminology. Furthermore, as a basis for understanding the objectives of zemiology, this chapter will outline the nine fundamental criticisms levelled toward criminology by Hillyard and Tombs (2008). In this chapter, some of the fundamental tensions between crime, criminology and social harm become apparent.

Moving on from the definitions and introductory examples given in Chapter 1, Chapter 2 focuses upon the areas of contention between criminology, critical criminology, social harm and zemiology. It pulls together some of the key responses to the early works established in *Beyond Criminology* (2004) to outline criticism from various academics working in the fields of criminology and critical criminology. The chapter also considers what we know about harm, and introduces some of its characteristics. Chapter 3 goes on to develop in-depth considerations of how harm itself is defined, and how dimensions of harms might be categorised heuristically. This is based upon the development of a tentative critical typology, exploring physical harms, emotional/psychological harms, economic and financial harms, cultural harms, harms of recognition and autonomy harms. While we set our apparently discrete categories, however, we emphasise that harms are experienced as multi-dimensional, are layered, have ripple effects and work themselves out synergistically.

Then, in Chapter 4, further focusing upon the contours and dynamics of the concept of social harm, we explore various ways in which harms need to be considered in relational terms – where harm is also always linked to benefit, whether this is for identifiable agents, institutions and interests, or for maintaining or exacerbating existent, unequal power structures. Then we review efforts to determine the ontology of harm. That review traverses in particular contributions made by Pemberton (2015), Yar (2012), Soliman (2019) and Raymen (2019), as a result of which we conclude that while there is clearly no agreed ontology of harm – there remains a great deal of conceptual work to be done here – there are nonetheless some key, emergent points of agreement on what the contours of such an ontology looks like.

Having explored social harms both conceptually and via dimensions of harm, Chapter 5 focuses on how this approach might be operationalised. Researching social harm often involves doing at least one of two things: exposing, documenting, mapping and understanding a harm or harms as they have been experienced *and* determining how they have been produced and are sustained. In this chapter we shall make some zemiological observations on these two – inter-related, of course – activities, – and then consider what they imply for counter-hegemonic practices. Then, relatedly, in our concluding chapter, we emphasise that zemiology must be a participative and co-operative activity, operating beyond academic borders – zemiology, we argue, must be embraced as an activist as well as an academic activity.

References

Ariadne Labs (2020) Emerging COVID-19 success story: South Korea learned the lessons of MERS, *Exemplars in Global Health*, 30 June, https://ourworldindata.org/covid-exemplar-south-korea, https://blacklivesmatter.com/black-lives-matter-global-network-responses-to-covid-19-ethnicity-data/, last accessed 18 August 2020.

Hillyard, P. and Tombs, S. (2008) Beyond criminology?, in *Criminal Obsessions: Why Harm Matters More Than Crime*, edited by D. Dorling, D. Gordon, P. Hillyard, C. Pantazis, S. Pemberton and S. Tombs, London: Centre for Crime and Justice Studies, 7–25.

Hillyard, P., Pantazis, C., Tombs, S. and Gordon, D., eds. (2004) *Beyond Criminology: Taking Harm Seriously*, London: Pluto Press.

Lorde, A. (2017) *The Master's Tools Will Never Dismantle the Master's House*, London: Penguin Classics.

Pearce, N., Lawlor, D. and Brickley, E. (2020) Comparisons between countries are essential for the control of COVID-19, *International Journal of Epidemiology*, 29 June, doi.org/10.1093/ije/dyaa108, last accessed 18 August 2020.

Pemberton, S. (2015) *Harmful Societies: Understanding Social Harm*, Bristol: Policy Press.

Pollack, T. *et al.* (2020) Emerging COVID-19 success story: Vietnam's commitment to containment, *Exemplars in Global Health*, 30 June, https://ourworldindata.org/covid-exemplar-vietnam, last accessed 18 August 2020.

Quality Assurance Agency (2014) *Subject Benchmark Statement: Criminology*, Gloucester: The Quality Assurance Agency for Higher Education.

Quality Assurance Agency (2019) *Subject Benchmark Statement: Criminology*, Gloucester: The Quality Assurance Agency for Higher Education.

Raymen, T. (2019) The enigma of social harm and the barrier of liberalism: Why zemiology needs a theory of the good, *Justice, Power and Resistance*, 3 (1), 134–163.

Soliman, F. (2019) States of exception, human rights and social harm: Towards a border zemiology, *Theoretical Criminology*, online first: 1–19.

Tombs, S. (2019) Grenfell: The unfolding dimensions of social harm, *Justice, Power and Resistance*, 3 (1), 61–88.

Tombs, S. (2020) Home as a site of state-corporate violence: Grenfell Tower, aetiologies and aftermaths, *Howard Journal of Crime and Justice*, 59 (2), 120–142.

Tombs, S. and Whyte, D. (2015) *The Corporate Criminal: Why Corporations Must Be Abolished*, Oxon: Routledge.

Wieler, L., Rexroth, U. and Gottschalk, R. (2020) Emerging COVID-19 success story: Germany's strong enabling environment, *Exemplars in Global Health*, 30 June, https://ourworldindata.org/covid-exemplar-germany

Witzany, G., ed. (2012) *Viruses: Essential Agents of Life*, Dordrecht: Springer Science.

Yar, M. (2012) Critical criminology, critical theory and social harm, in *New Directions in Criminological Theory*, edited by S. Hall and S. Winlow, London: Routledge, 52–65.

1

UNDERSTANDING SOCIAL HARM

Introduction

As we have highlighted, the key objective of this book is to create a platform for advancing the theoretical and empirical development of zemiology in ways which distinguish it clearly from criminology. Given this objective, it may seem rather contradictory to begin this story *within* the umbrella of criminology but, since the origins of zemiology itself were developed as a counteraction to what some considered to be the harms of mainstream criminology, then that is exactly where this chapter must begin. In a way, the story of zemiology might in fact go back one step further than the title of this book to look more like *From Criminology to Critical Criminology to Social Harm to Zemiology* – although we hope you will agree we opted for something slightly snappier!

This chapter therefore outlines the ways in which the study of social harm came to be developed in critical criminology, and how the two approaches might diverge. We will reflect on the key correlations and contentions within the approaches, and map the history of these as they developed, particularly through the 1990s and beyond. From this, we hope to situate a springboard from which the remainder of the book will move towards zemiology as a discipline in its own right: forged by the contentions it has met within and across criminology, but striving to create an alternative approach to seeing, evidencing, understanding and thus mitigating systemic social harms.

Haunted by 'the criminal man'?

Contemporary societies are awash with images, representations, discourses and claims around 'crime' and 'criminals' – each of which is, either explicitly or implicitly, a contribution to understandings of what crime *is* and who the criminals *are*. This, at the same time, constructs, challenges and reproduces understandings of what is *not* crime and who is *not* the criminal.

Within the story of crime with which you will be most familiar, the criminal will likely be a young male, possibly from a Black, Asian or Refugee background. Such a stereotype is, of course, easily contradicted – but as is often the case with stereotypes, it has some relationship to reality. This reality relates strongly to two points: first, mechanisms of social control through processes of criminalisation disproportionately focus on poorer, Black and structurally disenfranchised groups. Second, there remains a lack of focus on harms or criminalised activities which are perpetrated by states, corporations or political elites. In short, with few exceptions, the gaze of law and law enforcement (and, in particular, policing) is seldom trained on the actions of those who are most powerful in society, but strongly concentrated upon regulating and criminalising those who are more marginalised.

Often the study of criminological theory begins with one of the founders of the discipline, Cesare Lombroso, an Italian, who published what is widely regarded as the first ever book in criminology – *L'Uomo Delinquente* (*The Criminal Man*) – in 1876. One of the most well-known aspects of his work claimed to identify the criminal type, not least through physical features – whether these be eyes that were set close together, oddly shaped foreheads or jaws, noses that were flattened or twisted, and so on. For Lombroso, these features reveal something about individuals – that they possess abnormal or pathological genes, which in turn predispose those individuals towards criminality. In Lombroso's own terms, certain physical characteristics are the physical manifestations of 'atavism', marking throwbacks to a more primitive stage of human development, inferior physically and also psychologically to 'normal' citizens – citizens not infected with the pathological genes.

All of this might sound a bit far-fetched to contemporary criminology. Is it really feasible to identify an internal abnormality or pathology just by someone's physical features? Is there really a condition called atavism that means that some people are less developed than others? Perhaps unsurprisingly, in general, budding criminologists quickly learn the criticisms of these claims and move on from them as if they are so outlandish that they have no resonance within our understandings of crime, criminality and the criminal. Crime is not the product of a genetic condition, an abnormality, an illness – surely things are much more complex than that?

Lombroso's theory, as with much criminological theory, was a product of a specific historical, political and social context: Italy's unification into a nation state. His ideas mirrored a broader discourse to explain the different economic trajectories of the north and south of Italy with northerners seen as entrepreneurs and southerners as lazy, a discourse which provided an official justification for the expropriation of southern wealth and the violence meted out to those who resisted unification. However, it may not be wise to be so immediately dismissive of Lombroso in one respect: his claims that criminals look different are, if not accepted in detail, certainly coherent with popular representations of 'the criminal', and indeed match up to some vague idea or image that people somehow both recognise and act upon in their daily lives. Perhaps something like the image you hold in your mind's eye if asked to picture a 'criminal'?

Have you ever heard, said or thought the phrase, 'he doesn't look the type'? Who has not made assumptions about a group of young people based upon their being gathered in a public place, dressed in a certain manner? Perhaps you have crossed the street or decided not to sit in a certain spot on public transport because of the way someone looked – the *type* they seemed to be? None of this necessarily implies being discriminatory, but it does mean that all of us 'grow up' with stories of what crime and who the criminal is which are very powerful indeed. Moreover, some of the same ideologies used by Lombroso are still employed in criminal justice approaches. The most obvious example of this is the worrying re-emergence of 'neuroscientific' investigations of brain scanning of 'potential terrorists' – based on approaching Muslim men for such an activity, thus relying on a social construct of potential deviance (hence our comparison to Lombroso – for more information see Hamid and Pretus, 2019).

However, to think a little more outside the human box, let us walk through the application of such physical attributes towards behaviour as per undertaken in the policing of so-called 'dangerous dogs'.

Case study example: policing dangerous dogs, Lombroso style

Breed Specific Legislation (BSL) is a form of legislation aimed at controlling the ownership and reproduction of certain breeds of dog. At the time of writing, there are 52 countries which exercise some form of BSL. BSL was originally developed in the early 1990s in response to various high-profile cases of dog-related deaths of children. The most common breed regulated was initially the American Pitbull Terrier, expanding to encompass in some countries 'pitbull-type breeds'. In the UK, for example, this extends to include also the Japanese Tosa, Fila Braziliero and Dogo Argentina. In Denmark, this banned list extends to 25 breeds, as well as crossbreeds thereof. As the Royal Society for the Prevention of Cruelty to Animals notes,

> The term pit bull is an elastic, imprecise and subjective phrase ranging from the American pit bull terrier breed at its narrowest end through to a term which includes a number of bull breeds. It is also used to describe dogs similar in appearance e.g. block heads, white chest markings or brindle coats.
>
> *(RSPCA, 2016: 8)*

Ironically then, the most common dog breed regulated by BSL is not a breed *per se*, but a culmination of breeds and cross breeds!

This leads us to think about ways in which biological essentialism – which considers deviant or criminal (and other) behaviours to be the product of physical characteristics – plays out in the regulation of BSL. Take a look at the below list of criteria (Box 1.1) used by police in the UK – devised originally by the American Dog Breeders Association to determine the physical attributes of the Pitbull.

What becomes obvious here is that determining most of these attributes is an exercise in subjectivity. Can you define a small and deep-set eye? What is a 'good depth' from the top of a head to the bottom of a jaw? What is an 'athletic appearance'? When we see this in these terms, the parallels with Lombroso's atavistic man – determined by cranial shape and lesions, forearms and so on – it becomes clear that depending on body shape and size is perhaps not the most effective way of linking physical attributes to behaviour, either in humans or animals.

At this point you might wonder what on earth dog behaviour has to do with a move towards researching from a zemiological perspective. However, it is here that the nuance of zemiology can be applied in the context of both investigating and thus addressing, harm.

First, BSL is based on the assumption that a problem in society, in this case injuries caused by dogs, can be regulated by illegalising specific breeds based on physical characteristics. A zemiologist would reject such essentialism and consider instead what harms are inflicted by such interventions, and indeed if such approaches actually mitigate the serious harm in question. To the former, all evidence suggests that no, we cannot determine behaviour based on physical attributes. Although we can predict the potential impact of a bite in terms of ratio to the dog and jaw, whether or not a dog bites is not connected to its ability to do so (which dogs do not know) but to the way in which is it socialised and treated. Indeed, in a survey of 215 leading behaviourists undertaken by Battersea Dogs & Cats Home in the UK, 74

BOX 1.1 OUTLINE OF CHARACTERISTICS EXPECTED OF 'PITBULL TYPE DOGS'

- When first viewing the dog it should appear square from the side,and its height to the top of its shoulders should be the same distance as from the front of its shoulder to the real point of its hip.
- Its height to weight ratio should be in proportion.
- Its coat should be short and bristled,(Single Coated).
- Its head should appear to be wedge shaped when viewed from the side and top but rounded when viewed from the front. The head should be around 2/3 Width of shoulders and 25 percent Wider at cheeks than at the base of the skull (this is due to the cheek muscles)
- The distance from the back of the head to between the eyes should be equal to the distance from between the eyes to the tip of its nose.
- The dog should have a good depth from the top of head to bottom of jaw and a straight box-like muzzle.
- Its eyes should be small and deep-set. triangular Whan viewed from the side and elliptical from front.
- Its shoulders should be wider than the rib cage at the eighth rib.
- Its elbows should be flat with its front legs running parallel to the spine.
- Its forelegs should be heavy and solid and nearly twice the thickness of the hind legs just below the hock.
- The rib cage should be deep and spring straight out from the spine, it should be elliptical in cross section tapering tapering at the bottom and not 'barrel' chested.
- It should have a tail that hangs down like an old fashioned 'pump handle' to around the hock_it should have a broad hip that allows good attachment of muscles in the hindquarters and hind legs.
- Its knee joint should be in the upper third of the dog's rear leg, and the bones below that should appear light, fine and springy.
- Overall the dog should have an athletic appearance, the standard makes no mention of ears, colour, height, or weight.

(DEFRA, 2009: 20)

per cent said that breed was either not at all or only slightly important as a reason for why dogs attack people, while 86 per cent said that how the dog was brought up by the keeper was very important (Battersea Dogs and Cats Home, 2016). To the latter point, BSL is ineffective at addressing the harm caused by dog-related injuries. It has not reduced dog bites, which are on the contrary *increasing* even after almost 30 years of BSL in the UK (RSPCA, 2016: 14). Despite this, state institutions continue to implement the same approach and in doing so expand the role of the process of policing and punishment.

Focusing again on deaths, as the RSPCA highlights, in the UK 30 people died in dog-related incidents between 1991 and 2016, a minority (9) of which involved dogs registered as one of the four dangerous 'breeds' (RSPCA, 2016: 3). As such, the characteristics determined in the above list become increasingly irrelevant. From a zemiological perspective, these 30 deaths are not insignificant: death causes harm to and beyond the individual, and preventable deaths (as most dog-related deaths are, through training and behavioural intervention) are cause for serious concern. However, when we compare this number of people to those who have died in the UK due to excess winter deaths discussed in Chapter 2 as an example, we can see that responses much more proactive regarding regulation and policing of breeds despite the much higher number of people dying from cold. Moreover, research by the organisation *Born Innocent* found that the majority of dogs destroyed in the UK after being seized under the Dangerous Dogs Act 1991 had not exhibited any dangerous behaviour or been involved in any incident with the public. The latest available figures show that in 2015/2016 a total of 307 dogs were destroyed in just one year after being seized, but that 175 of these (57 percent) would be widely regarded as 'innocent' (Sawer and Scott, 2018).

This brings us to think about the dimensions of harm inherent to BSL. As we shall see in Chapter 3, we can identify various types of harm here, including physical harm (to the dog), and cultural harm (through misrecognition of breeds). Importantly, as the RSPCA recognises and as Lawson has found (Lawson, 2019), BSL causes significant levels of emotional and psychological harm to the keepers and families of dogs seized under BSL. In its report, it evidences cases of depression, anxiety, loneliness, self-blame, grief and loss. These are significant impacts for people to live with and – given the number of dogs seized per year as above – in no small numbers, thus compounding the harm of the problem of dogs. For aggressive dogs, rather than alleviate the anxieties or frustrations which can lead to unacceptable behaviour, being seized and held in kennels exacerbates the likelihood of problematic behaviours and thus actually increases the likelihood of causing further harm in the future! Moreover, who is policed under this legislation is strongly linked to class and in some areas racialisation processes, and so is not exempt from disproportionate impacts on already over-policed sectors of society – perpetuating certain myths of 'crime'.

There is no denying that injury or death caused by a dog is incredibly harmful for those affected, and so the possibility of this should be mitigated.

As we can see though, this is not done through BSL, but is much more likely through behavioural interventions. There is also no denying that some people within society use dogs for untoward and unacceptable activities, as 'status dogs' or for the abhorrent 'sport' of dog fighting. These points, however, are issues which connect much more deeply to power, violence, disproportionately violent masculinities and abuse – not the shape of an animal's head. As such, when we scrape the surface of how and why such legislation exists, we come to see that this kind of Lombrosian logic is as flawed for dogs as it has been for humans.

What is a 'criminal'?

What is meant when the word 'criminal' is used? For one thing, it's rarely a compliment – the term usually denotes someone who is bad or at least not *normal* in some way. The deviant, the outsider, the misfit, the offender are all terms that have been used interchangeably with the criminal.

Sometimes the word is used as if it completely defines someone: referring to someone as a criminal usually obscures the fact that they might also be a daughter, a parent, an employee, a member of a sports club, a university student – they may be all of these things, and more besides, with a past and a complex biography. But the word 'criminal' reduces someone, their whole identity, to the fact that they have been processed through the criminal justice system (CJS) or, to use a slightly different term, has been subject to criminalisation.

Possibly the term 'criminal' simply means those who have been formally processed through the CJS as having broken the criminal law – upon which we will focus on in Chapter 2. So what is known about these people? The short answer is – perhaps surprisingly – not very much. The one part of this group of people about whom something can be or is known are those who are imprisoned – by definition, prisoners are a captive audience, about whom basic data can be collected. In fact, when Lombroso studied criminals, one of the places he went to do so was the prison.

What we know about the prison population around the world is that it is overwhelmingly male, disproportionately with Black and/or Asian heritage, and relatively young. So, popular images of 'the criminal' may not be too far from reality if applied to *people in prison* rather than all criminals.

Case study: the unequal distribution of criminalisation and control

One such way of creating a snapshot insight into what we mean here is the case of England and Wales through the Bromley Briefings by the Prison

Reform Trust, a regular report which includes an outline of the demographics of people confined in prisons. By considering in this instance racial profiling, we can see that 'stereotypes' are not simply a mythology, but based in the unequal use of sanctions on specific demographics. For example:

- There is a clear direct association between ethnic group and the odds of receiving a custodial sentence. Black people are 53 per cent, Asian 55 per cent and 'other' [their word] ethnic groups 81 per cent more likely to be sent to prison for an indictable offence at the Crown Court, even when factoring in higher not-guilty plea rates.
- Black men are 26 per cent more likely than white men to be remanded in custody. They are also nearly 60 per cent more likely to plead not guilty.
- The number of Muslim prisoners has more than doubled over the past 17 years. In 2002 there were 5,502 Muslims in prison, by 2019 this had risen to 13,341. They now account for 16 per cent of the prison population, but just 5 per cent of the general population. (Prison Reform Trust, 2019: 24)

Similarly, the criminal activities with which we are most familiar are those upon which the police and criminal justice system overwhelmingly focus – inter-personal violence, theft, robbery, burglary, sexual assaults, taking and driving away, the use and sale of illegal drugs, perhaps shoplifting and cybercrimes. Again, this focus is not purely erroneous – but to see these offences as equating to 'the crime problem' is, as with the function of stereotypes of the criminal, to exaggerate, distort, obscure and mispresent reality.

Writing in 1982, Paul Gilroy focused on what he called 'the myth of black criminality'. This took various forms: at one extreme is the idea that certain ethnic communities were characterised by an essential anti-authoritarianism. At the other end of the spectrum is the fact the police and the criminal justice system disproportionately targeted young Black men. Both reinforced a relationship between 'race' (especially young Black men) and crime that had become significant in the UK through the 1970s. This was evident in a variety of ways. The 1970s and then 1980s saw: the emergence of the figure of the Black 'mugger'; inner-city disorders, where young men, predominantly African-Caribbean, confronted the police on the streets as a response either to racist policing; and the policing of Black cultural events (such as the Notting Hill carnival) classified as matters of public order.

One way of understanding the myth of Black criminality to which Gilroy pointed is through the systematic and disproportionate criminalisation of Black men. This is not simply an historic phenomenon. As indicated above,

People in prison

Social characteristics of adult prisoners

Characteristic	Prison population	General population
Taken into care as a child	24% (31% for women, 24% for men)	2%
Experienced abuse as a child	29% (53% for women, 27% for men)	20%
Observed violence in the home as a child	41% (50% for women, 40% for men)	14%
Regularly truant from school	59%	5.2% (England) and 4.8% (Wales)
Expelled or permanently excluded from school	42% (32% for women, 43% for men)	In 2005 >1% of school pupils were permanently excluded (England)
No qualifications	47%	15% of working age population
Unemployed in the four weeks before custody	68% (81% for women, 67% for men)	7.7% of the economically active population are unemployed
Never had a job	13%	3.9%
Homeless before entering custody	15%	4% have been homeless or in temporary accommodation
Have children under the age of 18	54%	Approximately 27% of the over 18 population*
Are young fathers (aged 18–20)	19%	4%
Have symptoms indicative of psychosis	16% (25% for women, 15% for men)	4%
Identified as suffering from both anxiety and depression	25% (49% for women, 23% for men)	15%
Have attempted suicide at some point	46% for women, 21% for men	6%
Have ever used Class A drugs	64%	13%
Drank alcohol every day in the four weeks before custody	22%	16% of men and 10% of women reported drinking on a daily basis

FIGURE 1.1 Social characteristics of adults in prison, Bromley Briefings, Winter 2019

Source: Prison Reform Trust (2019).

the over-representation of those from Black and Asian communities, as well as foreign nationals, in prison populations persists globally.

Indeed, when we unpick the surface of who is at the receiving end of punishment and social sanctions, a clearer picture emerges which alludes to racialised and social profiling. As abolitionist thinkers such as Bree Carlton, Angela Y. Davis and Ruth Gilmore Wilson have long documented, this picture of profiling the Black, Brown and indeed Indigenous and Aboriginal groups becomes clear the world over.

Likewise, as Figure 1.1 evidences, people held in prison in England and Wales (as in this example) are themselves significantly more likely to experience specific social hardships. This includes being more likely to have experienced more homelessness, alcohol dependency, unemployment or childhood abuse than the population more broadly. Entering prison is, therefore, associated with a cluster of other social harms – none which is to mention the fact that, as has been well documented, the experience of prison itself is an encounter with various forms of often highly degrading and dangerous social harms, which in their most extreme manifestations, in many nation states, end in considerable numbers of deaths whilst in custody (INQUEST, 2020).

In 2017 the British Government's Race Disparity Audit found that Black and Asian groups were much more likely to be unemployed, and to be excluded from school and so achieve poor educational qualifications (Cabinet Office, 2017) – and these characteristics tend to be associated with people who get caught up in the criminal justice system. But even taking all of these, and other, factors into consideration, there is a good case for saying that, in the UK, people from Black, Asian and Minority Ethnic (BAME)[1] populations get caught up with the police and the criminal justice system for the simple reason that they are not white Britons – that they are part of a BAME population. Thus it can be said that the criminal justice system, and its constituent parts such as the police and policing, are racialised – they operate systematically differently along racial and ethnic lines.

Thirty-five years after Gilroy's arguments, in 2017, the Labour MP David Lammy[1] oversaw a major review of 'the treatment of, and outcomes for Black, Asian and Minority Ethnic individuals in the criminal justice system' (Lammy, 2017a). The review documented how: racial discrimination permeated virtually every stage and process of the criminal justice system resulting in the disproportionate representation of BAME prisoners; the situation was getting worse; and in particular it was getting worse in the youth justice system, to the extent that the 'disproportionate number of BAME young people in the justice system is a social timebomb' (Lammy, 2017b).

More recently, in the UK, the racialised operation and effects of criminal justice processes and institutions have been at the heart of discussions amongst academics, practitioners, policy makers and politicians in the UK around a series of related criminal justice issues – gangs, drugs, violence and knife crime. These debates have centred on how to define a gang, whether gangs need to be understood in ethnic and racial terms, the extent to which gangs are disproportionately involved in certain kinds of violence, not least that involving guns and knives.

Many of these areas (gangs, violence, 'race' and ethnicity) come together in the legal doctrine of Joint Enterprise (JE), cases where more than one person is to be prosecuted for the same offence. Criminologists Becky Clarke and Patrick Williams (2016) note the significant increase in the use of JE as a way of prosecuting cases of so-called gang violence leading to murder in the UK. They cite one study that found that "the proportion of Black/Black-British people serving custodial sentences for JE offences is 11 times greater than the proportion of the general population who are Black/Black British (37.2 per cent compared to 3.3 per cent)" (Clarke and Williams, 2016, p. 7). Clarke and Williams argue that the myth of the 'gang' is used to support JE prosecutions – which they term 'collective punishments' (p. 7) – and that these processes are highly racialised.

Clarke and Williams examined policing tactics and organisations dedicated to tackling gangs and gang violence in London, Manchester and Nottingham. In each of these cities, they found, consistently, that:

- police and prosecutors are more likely to seek to demonstrate BAME defendants are part of a JE by invoking gang membership than is the case with non-BAME white defendants;
- despite featuring heavily in gang databases, young BAME people are not responsible for most serious violence in their areas.

Thus they conclude that young BAME people end up on gang databases as a result of racialised policing practices, not because of the actual risk they in fact pose (Clarke and Williams, 2016).

Beyond 'crime'

As important as those whom our stories of crime identify as actual or potential offenders are those who are thereby excluded. Ingrained, common-sense ideas regarding the criminal do not include the restaurant or factory owner, nor the directors of road transport or food-processing companies, nor the high-ranking military officer or indeed the local doctor or General Practitioner. They won't include senior managers at one of the big supermarkets, or petrol companies nor, most likely, the companies themselves, represented by an HQ building, a corporate logo, an organogram or a memorandum of incorporation, each of which would more accurately identify the origins of corporate-produced harm. But all of these individuals and abstract entities can (and do) act in ways that produce criminal outcomes – but they tend not to be conjured up by the word 'criminal'.

Of course, criminologists engage with and produce much more sophisticated stories of crime and criminals than these popular understandings. But criminology is neither immune from this general 'common-sense' approach, nor is it in control of it. Indeed, much criminological research is produced and maintained by very powerful interests, not least the state, which produces definitions of crime through criminal law, around which the whole edifice of punishment systems and their onlookers in the media, public and political spheres are then mobilised. In short, criminologists, like other people employed throughout the punishment process, have largely accepted a definition of crime as a violation of the criminal law, hence leaving the discipline hostage to a system that has criminalised individual behaviours like homosexuality and abortion, whilst minimising or overlooking harms generated through corporate activities such as tax avoidance or state atrocities such as genocide. And it is from this curious myopia that this book begins.

Contesting assumptions of 'crime'

As Hillyard and Tombs (2004a) noted, crime has no ontological reality. This means that the very basis of the use of the term 'crime' is fundamentally obscure: what we see or accept as 'crime' is not static, but can change across time and space. Take some of the below examples (Table 1.1):

As this shows, what is determined as a 'crime' changes considerably in relation to time and place. It is therefore not a 'natural' phenomenon, but one which is based in complex processes of law making and criminalisation. Importantly, the actions and processes defined as 'crime' are almost always defined and decided by those who are in positions of power – by political elites, dominated historically and contemporarily by middle and upper middle-class and higher caste men, as well as oligarchs and royal elites. If we accept socio-legal definitions of crime, then by default we have a tendency to explore problematic behaviours which are caused – and often disproportionately experienced – by people who are poor, working class and who experience relatively low levels of political power. We tend to focus on crimes of the powerless rather than actions, inactions or omissions which are more likely to harm, injure or kill us.

Now, many criminologists have long recognised, and struggled with, the inherent limitations of a state-based definition of crime. Sellin (1938), for example, suggested the alternative notion of 'conduct norms'. Sutherland (1945) famously extended the label 'crime' to those acts prohibited by bodies of law beyond the criminal law, illustrating "divergence between legal, social and political definitions of criminality" and thus reminding us "of the artificiality of all definitions of crime" (Nelken, 1994: 366). Using a human rights framework, Schwendinger and Schwendinger (1970) proposed that the harms arising from racism, sexism and economic exploitation should be central to the study of criminology. From a feminist perspective, Howe argued that harms against women were better understood if conceptualised

TABLE 1.1 Examples of 'crime' across time and space

Same sex relationships	As of 2019, 70 countries have outlawed same sex relationships. This means having a same sex relationship in any of these countries is deemed a crime. In countries such as Brunei and Saudi Arabia, people identifying as Lesbian, Gay, Bisexual, Queer or Intersex can be stoned to death, which would itself be a crime in many other countries.
Abortion	Abortion is illegal in many countries. However, taking Ireland as a case study, we can see the complexity of time and space where illegalisation is concerned. In 2018, the Republic of Ireland voted to legalise abortion until the 12th week of pregnancy. As such, women who chose to terminate a pregnancy in the Republic prior to 20th December 2018 were engaging in 'crime'. Women who did so in Northern Ireland – just across an almost invisible border – continued to be criminalised until the end of 2019.
Death penalty	Under the Universal Declaration of Human Rights (1948) all people have a right to life (Article 3). It is generally agreed that killing another human being is a particularly heinous 'crime'. However, although most countries have abolished the death penalty, more than 60 percent of the world's population live in countries where the state has the right to kill citizens under the death penalty. As such, even within states, the same action (i.e. killing a human) can be defined as a crime if undertaken by a citizen or through extrajudicial killing, but legal if sanctioned by the state in countries where it has been deemed legal through the criminal justice system, even though the outcome (loss of life) is the same.

as social injuries, experienced endemically by women as a subjugated group. For Michalowski (1985: 317), illegal or harmful acts that arise from the ownership or management of capital, which he calls 'crimes of capital', should also be studied within the discipline. More recently, Tifft and Sullivan (2001: 191) sought to extend the definition of crime to include, "social conditions, social arrangements, or actions of intent or indifference that interfere with the fulfilment of fundamental needs and obstruct the spontaneous unfolding of human potential". Notwithstanding these, and other efforts, by the turn of this century, "the concept of social harm" had "never seriously been incorporated into criminology" (Muncie, 2000: 3–9). At the same time, whether consciously or not, criminology had separated off and colonised specific categories of harms – crimes, defined by law – and therefore their supposed mitigation lay within criminal sanction processes. This tended either to obscure or to treat as unnecessary and eradicable side-effects the harms produced by those very processes – so, for example, reforming the punitiveness of prisons by seeking to embed restorative justice practices within some of them ultimately had bolstered the prison and the criminal justice system *per se*, whilst undermining the potential efficacy of radical alternatives to them.

This prompted more fundamental thinking about how a concept of social harm could be more progressively developed as an alternative to crime and criminology. The motivations or routes via which individuals joined this conversation were various. Some were pursuing the conceptual struggles of Sellin, Sutherland and others to operationalise a concept of crime in their respective areas of work, where a lack of definitional and legal clarity, and indeed relative *non*-criminalisation, were the norm – notably those working on corporate, state and white-collar crime. Others approached this enterprise on the basis of a concern with the marked expansion of criminology as a discipline and the concomitant increase in the number of degree courses in British and Irish universities, while already established subjects, such as social policy and sociology, were declining. Some of this group felt that the notion of social harm could be developed at the margins of criminology, through challenging the discursive power of concepts of crime, 'criminal' and 'criminal justice'. For others, given the integral nature of these latter concepts to the discipline of criminology itself, any sustained focus on social harm could only be achieved within a new and separate discipline.

An outcome of these discussions was speculative consideration of a sustained focus on the study of social harm, or the development of an alternative discipline, zemiology. The word was adopted in 1998 from the Greek word for harm, *xemia*, during the Annual Conference of the European Group for the Study of Deviance and Social Control on the Greek island of Spetses. The aim was to establish a new word in an attempt to ditch the baggage of the formulations of crime, criminal justice and criminalisation – terms of previous social formations which became articulated as the dominant form of dealing with harms in nation states with their focus on the individual rather than on structures and ideologies. The challenge in using a constructed word, which was not yet in the dictionary, was to think anew about social harms and responses to them, increasingly produced by the profit-driven, unaccountable, non-criminalised destructive harms of the global capitalism – harms which were being increasingly assumed to be legitimate subjects for criminology to study.

Months after the 'naming' of zemiology, a conference, *Zemiology: Beyond Criminology?* was held in Dartington, England. It included a diverse range of contributions from academics, policy makers and practitioners, from a range of disciplines, including criminal justice, development economics and development studies, geosciences, law, poverty studies, public health, social policy, and sociology, with criminology being a decidedly minority presence.[2] Subsequently, some of these papers, along with commissioned essays, were published as *Beyond Criminology: Taking Harm Seriously* (Hillyard *et al.*, 2004).

Beyond Criminology was an eclectic, somewhat contradictory work reflecting a wide variety of contributors, theoretical positions, and levels and objects of analysis. The next section of this chapter reviews some of the central arguments in the challenge entailed in that book's title.

Beyond criminology

The starting point of *Beyond Criminology* was an elaboration upon nine fundamental criticisms of the discipline of criminology (Hillyard and Tombs, 2004a). These were fundamental in two senses: first, the authors believed them to be significant; second, they were the basis for the considerations that followed throughout the book about the relative merits of social harm and zemiology, as a development of or an alternative to criminology. These nine criticisms can be briefly summarised:

Crime has no ontological reality. There is nothing intrinsic in any behaviour that allows us to know that it is a crime without reference to an external index – namely, criminal law. It is in fact difficult if not impossible to conceive of any act that in all circumstances, in all places, at all times, appears as a crime. The taking of life, the expropriation of another's property and the deprivation of liberty all take legal forms. Crime is thus a 'myth' of everyday life, albeit a highly salient one. To be clear, to say that crime has no ontological reality (Becker, 1967; Box, 1983; Christie, 1994; De Haan, 1996; Hulsman, 1986; Mathiesen, 1974; Steinert, 1986) is not "a dismissal of crime as a 'fictive event'" – it is simply to recognise that its status as a reality is one that is constructed (and indeed can only be understood) within any given set of social relations, a complex which is always "contingent rather than necessary" (Lasslett, 2010: 2). We know that the different ways in which crime is constructed means that someone conducting the same act on successive days may be a criminal on one, a law-abiding person on another – depending on whether a criminal offence has been introduced or (less likely) removed overnight; similarly, she can be an offender and not on the same day by carrying out the same act in two different jurisdictions. Now, these simple observations have real import. They mean, for us, that some of the central elements of criminology make little sense. One can seek to understand how and why certain acts and actors are subject to criminalisation (or not), with what consequences, in which interests, how changes in the processes occur, and so on. But it does not really make sense to think about why 'crime' occurs, 'goes up', 'goes down', what deters or contributes to crime and criminality and so on; or, if it does, it only makes sense in a highly circumscribed and qualified way – but such circumscription and qualification tends not to characterise how the juggernaut of academic criminology proceeds.

Criminology perpetuates the myth of crime. In the large and exponentially growing criminological literature, with a few notable exceptions, criminologists typically take crime as an unproblematic concept and there is little or no attempt to offer a definition. Somewhat differently, where there is a consideration such as 'what is crime', this tends to be ritualistic, going-through-the-motions so that the authors or contributors to the edited collection can then get on with the real job of criminology – which is to offer theories about why people commit crime, about how crime should be measured, about how crime might be prevented or responded to without any discussion of the concept. Criminology may occasionally nod to its lack of ontological foundation but proceeds for the overwhelming part as if this is not an issue.

Crime consists of many petty events. Most crimes in popular consciousness are perceived as very harmful of events. Yet most behaviours which are defined as crimes are relatively harmless. They would not, as Hulsman (1986) noted, score particularly highly on a scale of personal hardship. Reiman argues in his 'pyrrhic defeat theory' of criminal justice policy and system, "the definitions of crime in the criminal law do not reflect the only or the most dangerous of antisocial behaviours" (1998: 61). He goes on to argue that neither do the decisions on whom to arrest or charge or the resulting convictions reflect the only or the most dangerous behaviours. Indeed, the fact that crimes cover such a wide range of effects, from the serious (harmful) to the petty (harmless), is one of the reasons why in both professional and academic contexts, harm or severity indices of crimes are increasingly prevalent (Ashby, 2017; Curtis-Ham and Walton, 2017).

Crime excludes many serious harms. By contrast, the criminal law often fails to embrace many serious harmful behaviours or, if it does, they are ignored or handled without resort to it. The two most obvious examples are, first, violence against women (VAW) and, second, corporate crime and state crime.

The United Nations determines Violence Against Women to be:

> any act of gender-based violence that results in, or is likely to result in, physical, sexual, or psychological harm or suffering to women,

> including threats of such acts, coercion or arbitrary deprivation of liberty, whether occurring in public or private life.
>
> *(United Nations, 1993)*

This broad encompassing definition has been a welcome development in recognising, naming and responding to violence against women – a social issue which is both endemic and systemic worldwide. UN Women, for example highlights estimates showing that:

- 35 per cent of women worldwide have experienced either physical and/or sexual intimate partner violence or sexual violence by a non-partner (not including sexual harassment) at some point in their lives. However, some national studies show that up to 70 per cent of women have experienced physical and/or sexual violence from an intimate partner in their lifetime.
- Of the 87,000 women who were intentionally killed in 2017 globally, more than half (50,000; 58 per cent) were killed by intimate partners or family members, meaning that 137 women across the world are killed by a member of their own family every day. More than a third (30,000) of the women intentionally killed in 2017 were killed by their current or former intimate partner.
- Approximately 15 million adolescent girls (aged 15–19) worldwide have experienced forced sex (forced sexual intercourse or other sexual acts) at some point in their life.

(UN Women, 2019)

All evidence shows that violence against women is endemic. However, if and how states incorporate international definitions, or how well these are embedded in law, differs across time and region. Whilst some states have developed, for example, laws pertaining to coercive controls or online harassment, such regulations are not standard globally.

However, even with these developments in law and through criminal justice processes, built on rigorous efforts by pioneering feminists and rights activists and academics, such violence remains 'under the radar' in many criminal justice processes. Sexual violence has disproportionately high rates of attrition, even where whole systems have been built to work specifically with responding to sexual violence. Globally, the numbers of women being killed by male partners or former partner – as addressed above – are relatively stagnant, including the United Kingdom where laws have developed exponentially to embed and address intimate partner violence. Moreover – as we will outline more fully in Chapter 5 – we are reluctant to consider that responses to violence against women are best placed within criminal justice. Apart from the clear point that no fewer women seem to be dying at the hands of men year in and out, nor are fewer subjected to sexual violence, survivors of violence often refer to the process of justice as itself harmful. Furthermore, since prisons are a place of inherent violence through confinement, we prefer to advocate other ways to address such endemic abuses from beyond criminal justice.

Second, corporate and state crimes. These are generally far more harmful than almost any form of conventional crime for some very obvious reasons. The scale of state and corporate organisations, their ambit, the numbers of people they can affect, and so on, means they can affect many, many more people – corporate 'mis-selling' generates illegal profits of billions of pounds (for example, through illegal sales of endowment mortgage or pensions schemes), while states can and do sponsor genocide. Indeed, some might say that the focus on events that are defined as crimes serves to distract attention away from the more serious harmful behaviours – creating a "carnival mirror image of crime" (Reiman, 1998). As Tifft and Sullivan (1980: 6) argue, "by insisting on legal assumptions as sacred, criminologists comply in the concealment and distortion of the reality of social harms", particularly those harms inflicted by persons with power.

Constructing crimes. The construction of a crime involves a number of complex and elaborate processes. For example, central to determining guilt is the concept of '*mens rea*' (the guilty mind) which applies principally, but not exclusively, to the individual. This involves a series of legal processes, artificial, proxy measures whereby intention has to be judged by examining a person's words and deeds, then speculatively assessing these against the standard: a fictitious ordinary person. This fixation with the guilty mind also reflects the individualistic basis upon which bourgeois law has been constructed; this bias is evident in the difficulties of ascribing criminal liability upon collective entities such as the corporation, in turn under-pinning the effective decriminalisation of many of the socially destructive effects of corporate activity. Indeed, as the failings of the Corporate Homicide and Corporate Manslaughter Act (2007) in the UK indicate, even laws explicitly designed to achieve corporate liability through subverting legal principles such as *mens rea* still fall foul of law's reasoning about what *real* homicide and manslaughter look like (Hebert *et al.*, 2019).

Criminalisation and punishment. Once a behaviour or incident has been categorised as a possible crime, the whole process of criminalisation begins: arrest, prosecution, conviction, punishment. The state, as Christie (1977) has pointed out, indeed now increasingly corporations in many countries, appropriates the conflict and imposes punishment. To categorise and respond to harmful behaviours as criminal sets in train a process which is managed by state institutions, focusing on the offender not the victim nor the underlying conditions which may have produced the crime (Macnaughton-Smith, 1970). In so doing, states, and increasingly their corporate allies, tend to reproduce pain, harm, and indeed the likelihood of further crime, while such processes of criminalisation foreclose any other form of response to harmful behaviour other than more criminalisation.

Simultaneously, criminalisation and punishment generally operate quite differently with respect to powerful offenders. When states are consistently failing to meet their internationally agreed responsibilities with respect to, for example, 'asylum-seekers' or in terms of levels of air pollution, and even if they are called to account, there is no process of criminalisation or punishment. Or, where corporate actors are processed through the criminal justice system, again we tend not to think of these as criminals. And, indeed, even when punishment is applied, which in the case of corporations overwhelmingly means a fine, the levels of such punishments are generally derisory whilst in any case in fact dispersed to the innocent – workers, consumers and so on (Tombs, 2016).

'Crime control' is ineffective. Ironically, perhaps the greatest contribution of criminology has been to show that 'crime control' is ineffective, that is, fails in stated rationales of reducing crime, rehabilitating offenders, improving social safety and deterring widespread violations of law. The starkest evidence of failure is in relation to prison – the ultimate sanction in many 'liberal-democracies'. Mathiesen in his classic text *Prison on Trial* (1990) describes the prison as a 'fiasco' which cannot live up to any of the rationales stated for its existence. Somewhat differently, crime control is perhaps better understood as a form of conflict control, a criminal selectivity based upon the twin mechanisms of under- and over-criminalisation (Vegh Weis, 2018). Thus crime control – along with the category of crime upon which it is predicated – serves to maintain unequal power relations, warehouses surplus or problem populations (not least on racialised and class bases) and, increasingly in the neo-liberal era, is a mechanism for the generation of profit and transfer of wealth from the public to the private.

The category of crime, and therefore criminology which is largely organised around it, gives legitimacy to the expansion of 'crime control'. Crime control is now a large industry solving two major problems, as Christie (1994) noted: differential access to paid work and the uneven distribution of wealth. The industry provides profit and work while producing control of those who would otherwise cause trouble. It can expand effortlessly because crime dominates all social harm concerns. For Henry and Milovanovic conventional 'crime control' efforts fuel the engine of crime: "control interventions take criminal activity to new levels on investment and self-enclosed innovation"

(1996: x–xi). Much of the criminalisation process is autopoietic: the system itself produces crimes, such as resisting arrest, assisting an offender, defaulting on a fine or a civil order, or jumping bail, as a direct consequence of the initial intervention. The system therefore reproduces and maintains itself. Second, the state creates and perpetuates harm, harms to the individual and to her/his family which often far exceed the harm done by the alleged behaviour. Moreover, we consider that the role of some aspects of criminological expansionism – including in higher education and training academies – contributes to the perpetuation of this criminological industrial complex.

The category of crime serves to maintain power relations. Crime plays a fundamental role in modern societies in maintaining existing power relations: it facilitates the ignoring of the collective harmful behaviours of those in power through privileging individual acts; it disallows reference to structural determinants of harmful individual behaviour such as poverty or inequality; and it maintains and sustains the powerful corporate bodies in the crime control industry. Since its inception, criminology has enjoyed an intimate relationship with the powerful, a relationship determined largely by its failure to subject to critique the category of crime – and disciplinary agendas set by this – which has been handed down by the state, and around which the criminal justice system has been organised (Cohen, 1981; Foucault, 1980; Garland, 1992). Of course, the category of crime, not least through the socially progressive work of criminologists, has at times, fleetingly, sought to challenge such power relations – one might think of the work of feminist criminologists here, around domestic and sexual violence. But any progress ascribed to, or 'efficacy' claimed on behalf of, crime and criminal justice here is, as with all crimes, not only difficult to evidence – see above – but with respect to powerful offenders (men over women, white people over those of colour, corporations over workers, consumers and communities and states over their citizens) – is always fragile, tenuous, subject to push-back, and at the same time legitimates the whole class-based, racialized and patriarchal edifice that is criminal justice.

In the light of these nine fundamental criticisms, we reiterate the argument that criminology is a distorting discipline – one incapable, because of a framework delimited by an existing body of criminal law, of understanding and analysing a whole range of harmful events and activities.

Many criminologists would recognise and even agree with some or many of the above observations. Yet, just as we can all subject crime stories and crime talk to critique, exposing their myths, fallacies, even pure falsehoods, whether this be about the 'criminal type' or the 'crime problem', for example, this does not in and of itself undermine them. In other words, a key issue for us is *the power of crime discourse*. Such is its power that it virtually naturalises the idea that 'crime' captures the most important and most dangerous of all social harms that will affect us from the cradle to the grave, as well as our belief that the only response or most effective response to social harm is 'criminal justice' – even in the face of us 'knowing' otherwise to be the case. Moreover, just as many of the above observations would be accepted by many criminologists, virtually all criminology proceeds as if none were at all pertinent. To refer back to the illustration in the previous section, if we are looking for problematic situations, 'crime' looks the type; 'harm' does not. These beliefs about crime constitute what Gramsci (1971: 419–425) called 'common-sense' – constructed and reconstructed through pro-hegemonic forces, albeit that they are not, of course, immune from challenge. 'Social harm' and 'zemiology' represent challenges to this common-sense.

From crime to social harm

Criminology has made many attempts at moving beyond the formal legal definitions of crime. One most obvious resort to moving beyond crime is to focus upon violations of law other than the criminal law. Without entering into a definitional debate here regarding the appropriate use of the term 'crime' (one which has been tirelessly rehearsed since the exchanges between Sutherland and Tappan over 70 years ago), it has become common-place to use the term 'crime' to encompass violations of law other than criminal law, notably civil, administrative and regulatory law (Pearce and Tombs, 1998). Indeed, if perhaps more latterly, 'crime' has also been used to refer to violations of soft law such as 'standards' or 'codes of conduct' (typically as these apply to corporate actors, not least in their multinational forms; Bittle and Snider, 2013). Such efforts have considerable legitimacy, at least in critical criminological circles. So 'crime' can be extended to cover violations of a range of codes beyond the criminal law.

Moving slightly further are those who wish to embrace within their intellectual ambit those harms which are punish*able* but not punish*ed*. This commitment can, again, be traced back notably to the work of Edwin Sutherland, who sought to bring to centre-stage those acts and omissions by corporations and their senior executives which could and should in principle be incorporated within criminal justice processes and within the discipline of criminology – but which remain at best relatively marginal, at worst absent. Thus, in terms of the criminal justice system, he argued that most such violations of law remained non-criminalised, whilst his work during the 1940s was a 'call to arms' to criminologists to focus not simply on the crimes and incivilities of the relatively powerless, but equally to shift their gaze upwards, to focus on the crimes committed by the powerful, within corporate contexts (Tombs and Whyte, 2009). One example of this which we will examine at the end of Chapter 3 is in criminological approaches to illegalised migration. Whilst many aspects of migration are subject to criminalisation (Bosworth and Turnbull, 2015; Stumpf, 2006), such as working illegally or trafficking, many processes (such as immigration detention) sit outside the peripheries of criminal justice (Canning, 2018). Thus to apply the term crime rather than control or illegalisation distorts the social reality of a person's lived experience, labels them and adds opprobrium to their already desperate situation. Moreover, and again as we will see in some depth, it is often those whose movements across borders are illegalised who actually experience significant harms as a consequence. So 'crime' can be extended to a range of behaviours which have not been subjected to any formal processes of censure, to any due process.

A somewhat different approach to incorporating harms within the criminological purview is represented by longstanding and heterogeneous attempts to focus upon the harms produced *by* the activities of the criminal justice system (CJS) itself or, indeed, in a related variation, upon the harms associated with non-criminalisation, that is, the omissions of the CJS. For example, 'green' criminology frequently focuses upon legal pollution, or pollution which might be illegal but which is neither investigated nor detected. The strategy here is often to refer to the couplet 'crime *and harm*' (Corteen *et al.*, 2016; Large, 2018; Quality Assurance Agency, 2014, 2019).

Somewhat differently, some use the term 'social harm' *instead of* crime, blurring any distinction between the legal and illegal (Ruggiero, 2015), at times via an implicit or explicit reference to immorality, that is, to acts or omissions which are self-evidently harmful even if not proscribed by law (Monaghan and Prideaux, 2016).

Between these various strategies, one effect is to render invisible crimes visible (typified in Davies *et al.*, 2014), another to name 'new' forms of crime – notable examples here being the emergence of hate - (Jenness and Grattet, 2004) and eco- (Ellefsen *et al.*, 2012) crimes. Characterising much of what have become known as 'critical criminologies', the over-arching focus tends to be on the harms associated with a variety of processes of non/criminalisation, usually in ways which emphasise the maintenance or exacerbation of existing structures of power, whether these be viewed through the lens of class, gender and/or secularity, ethnicity and race, age or, indeed, via some form of intersectionality. Generally, such attempts are couched in a version of equality or social justice or both, albeit the bases for either of both claims vary significantly, and may be well or barely articulated.

A further, distinct approach to embracing the production of 'harm' within criminology has been a focus upon the generation of harms through legitimate markets which, through the goods or services produced therein, are associated with consequences resembling those produced through acts or omissions which are in fact criminalised. Here, we have particularly in mind the edited collections of Freudenberg (2014), Hills (1987) and Passas and Goodwin (2004) as exemplars. Each of these collections describes a series of markets – created and maintained by the state, not least through law – for essentially legal products despite the fact that they are either designed to, or necessarily generate in their use, wide-scale social harms, including, typically, agro-chemicals, arms, food, gambling, pharmaceuticals and tobacco (see also Hillyard and Tombs, 2004b, 44–51).

To be clear, to say that the production, distribution and sale of these goods is legal is not to claim that criminal law in particular, and legal regulation in general, does not intervene in such markets. If we take the international arms trade, for example, it is clear that the market in such goods is regulated by international agreements and national states themselves. Moreover, while these are market regulations, it is also clear that this is a context in which criminal law, both nationally and internationally, can and occasionally does intervene – whether this is in response to bribery and/or corruption to secure contracts, for example, or as a result of use outside of internationally agreed conventions which results in actual or potential violations of international human rights standards. So this is not a sphere from which law, let alone criminal law, is absent – yet it is a sphere which is relatively far removed from the concerns of much of what passes for criminology and what ends up in criminalisation processes.

Thus we have here at least four sets of relationships between crime and harm, steps on a journey which seek to incorporate within the ambit of crime 'harms' which on, a strict ('black-letter law') definition of crime do not belong therein. In summary, these are:

- the extension of 'crime' into other forms of legal violation, beyond the criminal law;
- considerations of harms which are formally punishable but not punished;
- the harms produced by criminal justice systems themselves – and, by implication, the category of crime and the discourses of criminology;
- moral critiques of non-criminalised harmful acts which are considered morally wrong if not legally so.

Each of these has long had salience within and around criminology – not least critical criminologies.

Understanding the developing trajectory of zemiology as a discipline in its own right requires a clear underpinning of its historical and intellectual origins. This chapter has sought to provide this, specifically in outlining contestations with criminology, including in its critical variants. So we do not deny the influence of critical criminology in shaping and framing zemiology. But we do advocate that zemiology develops as a separate discipline, one focused upon endemic and systemic harms, not least those completely unrelated to processes of criminalisation.

In particular, we argue that zemiology should attempt to develop in the following ways:

- First, it has the potential to be more coherent theoretically, as well as more comprehensive, encompassing a far wider range of the deleterious harms to people's welfare throughout their life.
- Second, the focus of such a discipline could be much broader than the specific harms experienced by individuals where the perpetuator had a 'guilty mind'. Zemiology can also include the harms experienced by individuals, households, family units and indeed communities from whatever source, even encompassing mass harms. As a starting point, we suggested a fourfold typology of harm: physical, financial, psychological and cultural/environmental, but we build and expand upon that in this text (see for example Chapter 3).
- Third, a focus on harm allows a much wider investigation into who or what might be responsible unrestricted by individualistic notions of responsibility.
- Fourth, it avoids the intellectual gymnastics which critical criminologists are often made to undertake in order to embrace a broader range of harms which are not justified by the limitations of the legal definition of crime.
- Finally, it creates the opportunity to consider a range of policy responses to reduce harm beyond the dominant, relatively easy, but ineffective response of criminalisation.

The primary motivations of zemiology are therefore to provide conceptual tools to focus on harms which are endemic, but that often pass unseen and indeed unregulated, and which are themselves often based in power imbalances and intersectional oppressions. This may at times relate to harm reduction where relevant to researchers, such as work in mitigating drug or alcohol related harms as well as workplace harms. But again, we see this as possible from *outside* the realms of traditional criminal justice practices, and toward structurally challenging societal inequalities and increasing workplace pressures which exacerbate such problems. With this in mind, we will begin to develop the epistemological and ontological bases of contemporary and future forms of zemiological study.

Notes

1 This is the term used in Lammy's report, however we do not consider it a term which ideally reflects the complexities or depth of ethnic heritage.
2 On the conference, see www.radstats.org.uk/no070/conference2.htm

References

Ashby, M. (2017) Comparing methods for measuring crime harm/severity, *Policing*, 12 (4), 439–454, doi:10.1093/police/pax049

Battersea Dogs and Cats Home (2016) *What's Breed Got to Do with It?* London: Battersea, www.bdch.org.uk/files/Dog-bites-whats-breed-got-to-do-with-it.pdf (Accessed 15 December 2020).

Becker, H. (1967) Whose side are we on? *Social Problems*, 14 (3), 239–247.

Bittle, S. and Snider, L. (2013) Examining the Ruggie Report: Can voluntary guidelines tame global capitalism?, *Critical Criminology*, 21 (2), 177–192.

Bosworth, M. and Turnbull, S. (2015) Immigration detention, punishment and the criminalisation of migration, in *The Routledge Handbook on Crime and International Migration*, edited by S. Pickering and J. Ham, Oxon: Routledge, 91–107.

Box, S. (1983) *Power, Crime and Mystification*, London: Tavistock.

Cabinet Office (2017) *Race Disparity Audit Summary Findings from the Ethnicity Facts and Figures website*, London: Cabinet Office, https://assets.publishing.service.gov.uk/government/uploads/system/uploads/attachment_data/file/686071/Revised_RDA_report_March_2018.pdf (Accessed 14 January 2020).

Canning, V. (2018) Zemiology at the border, in *Zemiology: Reconnecting Crime and Social Harm*, edited by A. Boukli and J. Kotze, Switzerland: Palgrave Macmillan, 183–203.

Christie, N. (1977) Conflicts as property, *British Journal of Criminology*, 17, 1–15.

Christie, N. (1994) *Crime Control as Industry: Towards Gulags, Western Style?*, London: Routledge.

Clarke, B. and Williams, P. (2016) *Dangerous Associations: Joint Enterprise, Gangs and Racism*, London: Centre for Crime and Justice Studies, www.crimeandjustice.org.uk/sites/crimeandjustice.org.uk/files/Dangerous%20assocations%20Joint%20Enterprise%20gangs%20and%20racism.pdf (Accessed 14 January 2020).

Cohen, S. (1981) Footprints in the sand: A further report on criminology and sociology of deviance in Britain, in *Crime and Society*, edited by M. Fitzgerald, G. McLennan and J. Pawson, London: Routledge and Open University Press, 220–247.

Corteen, K., Morley, S., Taylor, P. and Turner, J., eds. (2016) *A Companion to Crime, Harm and Victimisation*, Bristol: Policy Press.

Curtis-Ham, S. and Walton, D. (2017) The New Zealand Crime Harm Index: Quantifying harm using sentencing data, *Policing*, 12 (4), 455–467.

Davies, P., Francis, P. and Wyatt, T., eds. (2014) *Invisible Crimes and Social Harms*, Basingstoke: Palgrave Macmillan.

De Haan, W. (1996) Abolitionism and crime control, in *Criminological Perspectives: A Reader*, edited by J. Muncie, E. McLaughlin and M. Langan, London: Sage, 456–477.

Department for Environment, Food and Rural Affairs (2009) *Dangerous Dogs Law: Guidance for Enforcers*, London: DEFRA.

Ellefsen, R., Sollund, R. and Larsen, G., eds. (2012) *Eco-Global Crimes: Contemporary Problems and Future Challenges*, London: Routledge.

Foucault, M. (1980) Truth and power, in *Michel Foucault: Power/Knowledge: Selected Interviews and Other Writings, 1972–1977*, edited by C. Gordon, Brighton: Harvester Press, 109–133.

Freudenberg, N. (2014) *Lethal but Legal: Corporations, Consumption, and Protecting Public Health*, Oxford: Oxford University Press.

Garland, D. (1992) Criminological knowledge and its relation to power: Foucault's genealogy and criminology today, *British Journal of Criminology*, 32, 403–422.

Gilroy, P. (1982) The myth of black criminality, in *The Socialist Register*, edited by M. Eve and D. Musson, London: Merlin, 47–56.

Gramsci, A. (1971) *Selections from the Prison Notebooks of Antonio Gramsci*, edited and translated by Q. Hoare and G. Nowell Smith, London: Lawrence and Wishart.

Hamid, N. and Pretus, C. (2019) The neuroscience of terrorism: How we got a group of radicals to let us scan their brain, *The Conversation*, 12 June, https://theconversation.com/the-neuroscience-of-terrorism-how-we-convinced-a-group-of-radicals-to-let-us-scan-their-brains-114855 (Accessed 30 June 2020).

Hebert, J., Bittle, S. and Tombs, S. (2019) Obscuring corporate violence: Corporate manslaughter in action, *The Howard Journal*, 58 (4), 554–579.

Henry, S. and Milovanovic, D. (1996) *Constitutive Criminology: Beyond Postmodernism*, London: Sage.

Hills, S., ed. (1987) *Corporate Violence: Injury and Death for Profit*, New Jersey: Rowman & Littlefield.

Hillyard, P. and Tombs, S. (2004a) Beyond criminology?, in *Beyond Criminology: Taking Harm Seriously*, edited by P. Hillyard, C. Pantazis, S. Tombs and D. Gordon, London: Pluto Press, 10–29.

Hillyard, P. and Tombs, S. (2004b) Towards a political economy of harm: States, corporations and the production of inequality, in *Beyond Criminology: Taking Harm Seriously*, edited by P. Hillyard, C. Pantazis, S. Tombs and D. Gordon, London: Pluto Press, 30–54.

Hillyard, P., Pantazis, C., Tombs, S. and Gordon, D., eds. (2004) *Beyond Criminology: Taking Harm Seriously*, London: Pluto Press.

Hulsman, L. (1986) Critical criminology and the concept of crime, in *Abolitionism, Towards a Non-Repressive Approach to Crime*, edited by H. Bianchi and R. van Swaaningen, Amsterdam: Free University Press, 25–41.

INQUEST (2020) *Deaths in Prison: A National Scandal*, London: INQUEST.

Jenness, Valerie and Grattet, Ryken (2004) *Making Hate a Crime: From Social Movement to Law Enforcement*, New York: Russell Sage Foundation.

Lammy, David (2017a) *The Lammy Review: Final Report*, https://assets.publishing.service.gov.uk/government/uploads/system/uploads/attachment_data/file/643001/lammy-review-final-report.pdf (Accessed 14 January 2020).

Lammy, David (2017b) The racial bias in our justice system is creating a social timebomb, *The Guardian*, 8 September, www.theguardian.com/commentisfree/

2017/sep/08/david-lammy-review-bame-children-face-prejudice-flawed-criminal-justice-system (Accessed 14 January 2020).
Large, J. (2018) Spot the fashion victim(s): The importance of rethinking harm within the context of fashion counterfeiting, in *Zemiology: Reconnecting Crime and Social Harm*, edited by A. Boukli and J. Kotze, Switzerland: Palgrave Macmillan, 223–245.
Lasslett, K. (2010) Crime or social harm? A dialectical perspective, *Crime, Law and Social Change*, 54, 1–19.
Lawson, C. (2019) *Dogs and the Criminology of Control: A Case Study of Contemporary Policy Making in England and Wales*, PhD Thesis, Cardiff University.
Macnaughton-Smith, P. (1970) *What Is Crime and Why Do We Fight It*, Paper delivered to the Centre of Criminology, University of Toronto, Canada, 14 January.
Mathiesen, T. (1974) *The Politics of Abolition*, London: Martin Robertson.
Mathiesen, T. (1990) *Prison on Trial*, Winchester: Waterside Press.
Michalowski, R. (1985) *Order, Law and Crime*, New York: Random House.
Monaghan, M. and Prideaux, S. (2016) *State Crime and Immorality: The Corrupting Influence of the Powerful*, Bristol: Policy Press.
Muncie, J. (2000) Decriminalising criminology, *British Criminology Conference: Selected Proceedings*, 3, http://britsoccrim.org/volume3/010.pdf (Accessed 14 August 2020).
Nelken, D. (1994) White collar crime, in *The Oxford Handbook of Criminology*, edited by M. Maguire, R. Morgan and R. Reiner, Oxford: Clarendon Press, 355–392.
Passas, N. and Goodwin, N. R. (2004) *It's Legal but it Ain't Right: Harmful Social Consequences of Legal Industries*, Michigan: University of Michigan Press.
Pearce, F. and Tombs, S. (1998) *Toxic Capitalism: Corporate Crime and the Chemical Industry*, Aldershot: Ashgate.
Prison Reform Trust (2019) *Bromley Briefings Prison Factfile: Winter 2019*, Prison Reform Trust, www.prisonreformtrust.org.uk/Portals/0/Documents/Bromley%20Briefings/Winter%202019%20Factfile%20web.pdf (Accessed 10 February 2020).
Quality Assurance Agency (2014) *Subject Benchmark Statement: Criminology*, Gloucester: The Quality Assurance Agency for Higher Education.
Quality Assurance Agency (2019) *Subject Benchmark Statement: Criminology*, Gloucester: The Quality Assurance Agency for Higher Education.
Reiman, J. (1998) *The Rich Get Richer and the Poor Get Prison: Ideology, Class and Criminal Justice*, 5th ed., Boston: Allyn and Bacon.
Reiman, J. (2006) Book review of *Beyond Criminology: Taking Harm Seriously*, *British Journal of Criminology*, 46, 362–364.
RSPCA (2016) *Breed Specific Legislation: A Dog's Dinner*, London: RSPCA.
Ruggiero, V. (2015) Social harm and the vagaries of financial regulation in the UK, *International Journal for Crime, Justice and Social Democracy*, 4, 91–105.
Sawer, P. and Scott, P. (2018) Dozens of 'innocent' dogs being destroyed under Dangerous Dogs Act, new figures show, *The Telegraph*, 25 November, www.telegraph.co.uk/news/2018/11/25/dozens-innocent-dogs-destroyed-dangerous-dogs-act-new-figures/ (Accessed 11 June 2020).
Schwendinger, H. and Schwendinger, J. (1970) Defenders of order or guardians of human rights?, *Issues in Criminology*, 5, 123–157.

Sellin, T. (1938) *Culture Conflict and Crime*, New York: Social Science Research Council.

Steinert, H. (1986) Beyond crime and punishment, *Contemporary Crises*, 10, 21–38.

Stumpf, J. (2006) The crimmigration crisis: Immigrants, crime and sovereign power, *American University Law Review*, 52 (2), 367–419.

Sutherland, E. (1945) Is 'white-collar crime' crime?, *American Sociological Review*, 10, 132–139.

Tifft, L. and Sullivan, D. C. (1980) *The Struggle to Be Human: Crime, Criminology and Anarchism*, Sanday, Orkney: Cienfuegos Press.

Tifft, L. and Sullivan, D. C. (2001) A needs based social harm definition of crime, in *What Is Crime? Controversies over the Nature of Crime and What to Do About It*, edited by S. Henry and M. Lanier, Lanham, MD: Rowman & Littlefield, 179–203.

Tombs, S. (2016) *Social Protection After the Crisis: Regulation without Enforcement*, Bristol: Policy Press.

Tombs, S. and Whyte, D. (2009) Corporate crime? Theft, violence and harm, in *Crime: Local and Global*, edited by J. Muncie, D. Talbot and R. Walters, Cullompton: Willan/ Open University Press, 137–172.

UN Women (2019) Facts and figures: Ending violence against women, www.unwomen.org/en/what-we-do/ending-violence-against-women/facts-and-figures (Accessed 10 February 2020).

United Nations (1993) Declaration on the Elimination of Violence Against Women, www.ohchr.org/en/professionalinterest/pages/violenceagainstwomen.aspx (Accessed 10 February 2020).

Vegh Weis, V. (2018) *Marxism and Criminology: A History of Criminal Selectivity*, Chicago: Haymarket Books.

2
TOWARDS SOCIAL HARM AND ZEMIOLOGY

Introduction

In Chapter 1 we charted how discussions in the late 1990s began to consider how a concept of social harm could be developed as a more progressive alternative to crime. We emphasised that the motivations or routes via which individuals joined these conversations were various, but that these developed into the book *Beyond Criminology: Taking Harm Seriously* (Hillyard *et al.*, 2004). And although it was in these discussions and the 2004 book that the study of zemiology began to take shape academically, it was these very different routes into, and commitments for having, these discussions, which helps to explain the lack of clarity about what social harm and zemiology might be, as opposed to what they were claimed *not* to be.

This chapter focuses upon some key areas of contention between criminology, critical criminology, social harm and zemiology. In the first part of the chapter, we pull together some of the key responses to the claims in *Beyond Criminology*, outlining criticism from various academics working in the fields of criminology and critical criminology. Then, in the latter half of the chapter, we begin to flesh out what we know about social harm and some of the bases upon which zemiology is founded and may be developed.

Beyond criminology – but to where?

In the latter half of the previous chapter, we set out to journey away from crime towards social harm, which could ultimately become a lengthy and significant one – albeit each of the specific steps 'beyond' criminology are, we suspect, possibly familiar to readers. And, we would go further: each seems to be a perfectly defensible, plausible and indeed productive way in which we can move from 'crime' to 'social harm'. In any case, what these various steps recognise is that there are a variety of relationships between 'crime' and 'harm' which inflect the work of criminologists.

But for some, not least some of the contributors to *Beyond Criminology*, the journey should not and does not stop here. By way of shorthand, each of the shifts from crime to harm set out previously revolves around the issues of the existence or level of criminalisation or non-criminalisation. But *Beyond Criminology* encompassed a series of harms associated with phenomena far from criminological and criminal justice agendas – including poverty, childhood, inequality, heterosexism, migration, gender, unemployment – and it is here that a new discipline of zemiology, the study of social harms, was being broached, however unconsciously in some specific cases. This is not to deny that many of these phenomena are relevant in understanding the definition and distribution of 'crime' and 'criminalisation', but it *is* to emphasise that many of the considerations around these in *Beyond Criminology* were not much or even at all about such issues. Criminology had, effectively, been abandoned.

Case study example: excess winter deaths

Each year, the UK's Office for National Statistics calculates the number of what are rather prosaically labelled 'Excess Winter Deaths' – namely, the additional number of deaths, in England and Wales, occurring from December to March compared with the average number of deaths occurring in the preceding and following four-month periods. The most recently (November 2019) published figure estimates 23,200 such deaths for the winter of 2018–2019 – the lowest recorded figure since 2013–2014. However, the Office for National Statistics recognises that year-by-year figures are subject to fluctuation and thus uses a five-year rolling average to determine trends – so that 2018–2019 is the third consecutive year in which an upward trend in Excess Winter Deaths in England and Wales had been recorded (Office for National Statistics, 2019).

Elsewhere we have considered various data sets which, we argue, clearly provide some bases for quantifying social harm, including data on work-related deaths, 'deaths brought forward' by environmental pollution and deaths associated with food poisoning (Tombs, 2016; Tombs and Whyte, 2015). Now, each of these phenomena has some proximate relationship to 'crime', criminalisation and criminal justice processes, in that each is regulated (at least partly) by criminal law, is subject to enforcement (albeit by regulatory bodies rather than, for the most part, police forces) and in any one year attracts a number of criminal prosecutions; moreover, the offences so prosecuted may revolve around intent or negligence or both, thus meeting standards of guilt in criminal law. Finally, it is worth noting that there are existent if small literatures around each in criminology.

Excess winter deaths are quite distinct in all of these respects. They are routine and mundane deaths, that is, they occur and are recorded every year, generally free from political, media, academic and popular scrutiny, but are socially preventable and social unnecessary deaths which could be and, in some societies, are avoided. Thus it is important to note that EWD are not deaths of people as a result of 'the cold' *per se* – a fact implied perhaps by the very reference to 'winter'. Table 2.1, for example, indicates that some European countries with very low winter temperatures – those in in Scandinavia and Northern Europe – have very low rates of such deaths.

Meanwhile, the fact that four of the top six countries in Table 2.1 are from warm, southern countries is attributable to "the excess winter mortality paradox" – that is, "people are more likely to die in such countries during cold snaps than in northern countries where winters are consistently severe" (Guertler and Smith, 2018: 10). Thus, "this more comparable measure of mortality in relation to cold conditions puts the UK second-worst (after Ireland) amongst 30 European countries" (Guertler and Smith, 2018: 2).

What this indicates, then, is that most deaths in the UK (and Ireland) result from lack of access to affordable heating, or suitably insulated, warm and dry accommodation, or most likely both (Office for National Statistics, 2019). In other words, their routine occurrence is a product of generations of decisions, actions and omissions regarding housing, energy, welfare and social services, health care and probably pensions policy, at the very least. Moreover, while each occurrence – a death – is an event, this event can only be understood in the context of the combination of a series of long-term *processes*. Little or none of these characteristics, and their inter-relationships, of what clearly amounts to a significant form of social harm, is *or can be* at all explicable via reference to criminal law – albeit some are clearly affected by regulatory law, not least in the creation then maintenance through and by states of complex markets in energy supply as well as in the regulation of some aspects of private provision of housing, some welfare services and pension provision.

Thus, harms such as excess winter deaths are nowhere near the terrain of crime nor encountered on the journey from 'crime' to 'social harm' as sketched out above. They are neither explicable nor preventable through criminal law, which seeks to view or reduce harm to intention, to the inter-personal, to the one or series of discrete events, to victim-offender relationships which have some proximity in time and space (Hillyard and Tombs, 2017). A focus

TABLE 2.1 Excess Winter Mortality (EWM) Index for 30 European countries

Country	*EWM index*	*Country*	*EWM Index*
Malta	29.4	Slovenia	13.2
Portugal	28.0	Hungary	12.3
Cyprus	23.6	Denmark	12.2
Spain	20.6	norway	12.1
Ireland	19.7	The Netherlands	11.8
UK	18.6	Germany	11.7
Greece	17.9	poland	11.7
Bulgaria	17.8	Latvia	11.5
Romania	17.5	Lithuania	11.5
Italy	16.0	luxembourg	11.2
Switzerand	14.2	Estonia	10.9
France	13.8	Czech Republic	10.8
Belgium	13.6	Finland	9.5
Sweden	13.3	Iceland	8.4
Austria	13.2	Slovakia	8.2

Source: Guertler and Smith (2018: 10).

on excess winter deaths takes us far beyond crime, criminalisation and criminal justice, far from criminal law and the orbit of mainstream criminology.

At this point it appears to us that the epistemological and ontological break with criminology is made – a break only illustrated, not theorised, here – but on which there will be more below. And it is here at which the terrain is crossed into a new discipline. Of course, whether this discipline can be something called 'zemiology' is a moot point. We shall return to that question shortly. But, for now, the above is enough to outline a claim, at least, that zemiology is or should be seen as something distinct from a 'social harm' perspective or approach – a claim never clearly asserted let alone established in *Beyond Criminology* nor, indeed, in some of the work which has followed and which has explicitly sought to develop the epistemological and ontological terrain very sketchily suggested in parts of that text.

The lacunae, tensions and indeed disagreements across the contributions to *Beyond Criminology* may do much to explain why an increasing number of criminological texts make explicit reference to the term 'zemiology' as simply synonymous with 'social harm' – the latter being a concept which has long been part of criminology, albeit one which has recently received greater attention (Muncie, 2013). Hence, the term zemiology has been happily embraced by many in the discipline – for example, *The Sage Dictionary of Criminology* (2013) contained an entry for 'Zemiology', which read thus: "See: Social harm" (McLaughlin and Muncie, 2013: 496). More generally, the embrace of 'social harm' has characterised much recent critical criminology, as we will outline in more depth as this chapter goes on.

Such positions/responses merely reproduce, perhaps exacerbate, the contradictions, confusions and disagreements that were present in *Beyond Criminology*. It is absolutely clear that in that collection, there was neither agreement on abandoning criminology for zemiology, nor what this might entail or might look like, nor on the relationship between criminology, zemiology and a focus on 'social harm'. If, at best, Hillyard and Tombs had set out some of the possible epistemological, theoretical and substantive commitments of zemiology as an alternative discipline, they did not attempt to set out in detail what that discipline might look like – a point which has been made by many since (Hughes, 2007; Loader and Sparks, 2011). Reiman, in particular, notes that taking "the next step ... from a provocative kaleidoscope to a coherent disciplinary perspective", entails at least two tasks: first, being "clear on the harm perspective's relationship to criminology" (Reiman, 2006: 363); and, second, since "so much of the harm discussed in *Beyond Criminology* is attributed to social groups or structures, the harm perspective will need to spell out a plausible doctrine of social or structural responsibility" (Reiman 2006: 364). These points are well made, and represent a significant challenge to those who would either develop a social harm perspective or an alternative discipline of zemiology.

Responses to the shift 'beyond' criminology

In this section, we focus first, briefly, on some dimensions of what we call the 'institutional' response to arguments for social harm and zemiology as intimated in *Beyond Criminology*, before discussing the substance of some of the 'intellectual' response. These terrains have, however, become very confusing because across them social harm and zemiology seem to have multiple meanings, not unlike Humpty Dumpty's dictum: 'When *I* use a word it means just what I choose it to mean – neither more nor less' (Carrol, 1934: 205, emphasis in original).

Criminology, as with any other discipline, is organised as a profession via a set of institutions, spanning associations and societies, conferences, symposia and seminars, a range of written publications, processes of formal accreditation and associated Higher Education provision, and so on. While we cannot quantify at all the various institutional responses, it is clear that social harm and/or zemiology have very quickly become an element of what constitutes the discipline, in a number of ways and at various levels. It is worth adding that this observation holds internationally, at least in the English-speaking academic world, and is not confined to the UK.

This is reflected in course and module content across undergraduate and postgraduate provision in UK universities. At least 14 UK universities run modules explicitly focusing on crime and/or social harm, as well as at least one in Sweden, one in Denmark and one in development in Slovenia. Numerous programmes now describe their criminology degrees as focusing also on social harm and provide social harm input at various stages throughout their respective programmes. This includes those institutions which offer criminology 'with' another discipline; indeed, where criminology meets social policy, there is clear evidence of an increasing focus on social harm. The University of Bristol, for example, offers a BSc in Social Policy with Criminology in which social harm figures prominently – perhaps not surprising, since the academics located in the School which offers the programme include Christina Pantazis (Professor of Zemiology) and Victoria Canning (co-author of this book).

The 'institutional' response of criminology has operated at other levels – in the form of criminological outputs, such as books and articles. Of the former, there is now small but growing literature on aspects of social harm and zemiology. Rob White's (2014) *Environmental Harm: An Eco-justice Perspective* was the first book to appear in a new series by Policy Press, entitled Studies in Social Harm, a book which was quickly followed by the ground-breaking *Harmful Societies: Understanding Social Harm* (Pemberton, 2015), on which more below. There are other books in this series – Scott (2017) and Lloyd (2018) – with several more in production. Beyond this particular series, other books have taken their central focus as social harm or zemiology – see, for example, Boukli and Kotzé, 2018; Canning, 2017; Davies *et al.*, 2014. One issue to note here upon which we will expand later is that social harm in the zemiological sense still rests predominately with scholars and activists in the Global North, with exceptions mainly in New Zealand and Australia, and even here this remains in the hands of predominately white scholars.

Recent years have seen special issues of criminological and socio-legal journals devoted to social harm, notably *Crime, Law and Social Change* in September 2007, the Journal of Global Indigeneity (3, 1, 2018) and two Special Issues of *Revista Crítica Penal y Poder* [Critical Review of Criminal Critique and Power] (issue numbers 4 and 6, in 2013 and 2014 respectively). More recently, two special editions of *Justice, Power and Resistance* have been published dedicated to different aspects of social harm – Pantazis *et al.* (2019) focusing on neo-liberal harm production and Mitchell *et al.* (2019) on culture, consumption and social harm respectively – while others have featured social harm centrally (*The Howard*

Journal of Criminal Justice, 54 (1); *State Crime*, Autumn, 3 (2)). In addition, it is now commonplace to see streams, panels and papers on social harm/zemiology at UK and international conferences and symposia.

The institutional response to *Beyond Criminology* has unsurprisingly come mainly from within criminology by expanding the thinking around the notion of social harm and embracing zemiology as *part of* criminology. However, a number of scholars working under the rubric 'beyond criminology' have, either explicitly or implicitly, adopted a social harm perspective to study an instructive variety of social phenomena. For example, work has been undertaken on the production of social harm in social care (Brogden and Nijhar, 2006; Phillips, 2007), in old age (Machniewski, 2010), the cut-flower industry (McGill, 2012), in the provision of new technology (Hope, 2013), in learning care settings (Feeley, 2014), and by corporations (Freudenberg, 2014; Passas and Goodwin, 2004). Somewhat differently, Presser (2013) has sought to develop a first attempt at a general theory of harm, based on four case studies – genocide, meat eating, intimate partner violence and penal harm. That said, focusing upon the narratives and discourses that support and perpetuate harm, her theoretical contribution is one around harm*ing* rather than harm *per se*.

There is no doubt that the focus of criminology has continued to expand – and that there is a significant body of critical criminological work with a healthy diversity of concerns. This may, of course, simply be an effect of the growth of the discipline, so that while there is more 'critical' work undertaken, its relative size compared to criminological output is no greater. In any case, the case remains: work conducted within the boundaries of criminology must ultimately confront the inherent limitations of working within the discipline – a point that is rarely, if ever, addressed in critical responses to the claims made in *Beyond Criminology*.

It is, however, an issue raised by others. For example, drawing on the work of Pavlich (1999) and Foucault (1977), Reece Walters has noted that, "some radical departures" within criminology find themselves "drawn back by the magnet of pragmatism in an attempt to be seen as 'useful' in preference to an idealistic and academic knowledge of little practical utility" (Walters, 2003: 39). Thus, he continues, "critical genres fail to question their historical and internal logics and thus continually run the risk of becoming fractured, fluid and susceptible to domination by conservative ideologies".

It was precisely such 'historical and internal logics' which Hillyard and Tombs (2004) sought to address through the work of Foucault (1977, 1979) on discursive formations. As Foucault showed us in these extensive writings, discourses define the reality of the social world, through its regimes of truth and none more so than what he described as the scurrilous discourses of criminology. Power and knowledge are not independent but intimately linked. Ideas which function as true are perpetuated by institutions and their discourses. Hence the need for a counter-discourse on social harm. This is precisely the issue that seems to be avoided by our critics.

A somewhat distinct, broad response has been to question the political project entailed in *Beyond Criminology*, in at least two senses: first, to advocate a continued commitment to reformism within and of criminology, and second to reject any exigence to abandon the discipline.

On the former, Maruna (2013) is clear: for him, criminal justice matters. It matters, for example, to those who are incarcerated – so the more criminologists studying prisons and proffering progressive reform, the better. Similar arguments were made regarding other criminal justice institutions, such as police, with the explicit statement that powerful institutions need to be studied. We agree wholeheartedly with this specific point (Tombs and Whyte, 2003), but ultimately it takes us back full circle to our starting place: it matters from where one studies these, or other, organisations. We also contend that the objectives of outcomes also matter: advising, for example, on how to make harmful practices less harmful (such as imprisonment or solitary confinement) are not conductive to the trajectory of structural changes in ending the harms inherent to their existence unless this is explicitly recognised in the research design and operation. In any case, for Maruna (2013), were criminology to be abolished and zemiology established in its place, there would be considerable pleasure among those critical of the 'left-wing' nature of the discipline. Such a claim rather begs the question of what it means to ascribe to the discipline a 'left-wing', and then what being a 'left-wing' criminologist can or does achieve. Further, and again, it fails to address the construction and limits of the discipline.

Criminology, then, needs to be defended (Maruna, 2013). It is wrong to blame criminology for the failure of the criminal justice system, just as it is illogical to blame historians for growing inequality in society. As Hughes (2007: 197) elaborates, zemiologists have taken "Foucault's typically magisterial" and "radical totalitarian" critique of criminology as proof of "criminology's sins, past and present". He goes on to suggest we argue that criminology, as the "handmaiden of the State", has a role in the "socially destructive trends of 'mass criminalization'".

On this basis, abandoning the discipline is a mistake. Better, says Hughes, to engage in "progressive alliance building" in order "to govern the soul of the criminological beast" (Hughes, 2007: 159, 158). Similarly, for Maruna, offering a thoroughgoing rejection of what counts for criminology, alongside an exigence to simply sign up to an alternative position, is a poor way to generate change. While there may be apparent plausibility to these observations, we are clear that, ultimately, criminology cannot change enough given the way in which it has been historically constructed, as a particular discursive formation, on which more below.

For Maruna, then, critics have a choice – either to exit the discipline, or to remain within criminology and express their criticisms from therein. The former, he claimed, was all too common within criminology and not very helpful because it was often the Left that exited leaving a more conservative group behind. This is not an unreasonable point to make, but it seems to us that it simply points to a political dilemma facing many who are members of organisations, be they political parties or academic disciplines. Carol Smart and Stan Cohen are well-known examples of key figures who explicitly abandoned the discipline – Smart with the later, reflective verdict that "the thing that criminology cannot do is deconstruct crime" (Smart, 1990: 77) – but anecdotally, many of us know colleagues who have done so also. As Muncie observes, "the abandonment of crime in favour of 'harm' is ultimately a political project" (Muncie, 2005: 201). On this point, with which we agree, we are taken back to our starting point, one aptly noted by Reiman, thus:

> Criminology, alone among recognized social sciences, bears the burden of having the object of its study determined by the state. We are accustomed to hearing about the politics of research, but this is the politicization of research with a vengeance. The result of it is that criminology bears a special responsibility: it must either declare its independence of the state or serve as an arm of the state.
>
> *(Reiman, 2006: 362)*

To be sure, many have moved away from state-centric funding, however as Reiman notes, this requires a declaration of independence, an issue which itself is subject to contrived notions of objectivity and subjectivity, a point to which we will return in Chapter 5, and also see Box 2.1.

Critical criminology, social harm and zemiology

In this substantive section, we argue that there are a number of fundamental theoretical differences between critical criminology, social harm and zemiology which help clarify the ongoing debates on whether zemiology should be considered as a separate discipline or simply a branch of critical criminology.

As we have indicated, criminology, and in particular critical criminology, has long struggled over the boundaries of the discipline in an attempt to shake off the limitations of the straightjacket of the legal definitions of crime

BOX 2.1 CO-AUTHOR'S NOTE: REFLECTIONS ON GENDER AND CRITIQUE BY VICTORIA

For anyone coming to this overview of critique with fresh eyes, you may be surprised to see that zemiology and the study of social harm more broadly seems dominated by men. This is particularly the case when presented with the myriad of critiques that has been levelled at zemiology, as this chapter explores in some depth.

However, it seems worth stating here that the discussions addressed by scholars in this chapter and later in Chapter 4 are almost exclusively discussions by men, about men and to men. Indeed, as we came to review literature for this book, it became increasingly obvious that many of these scholars have not stretched themselves to consider in much depth the vast array of empirical, conceptual and theoretical developments and offerings that have formed much of the basis of contemporary zemiology by women, trans and non-binary people (and which this book addresses). Indeed, in one chapter we read, two male professors outlined their position with a bibliography which included 47 references, encompassing 63 authors in all. Four of the authors/editors were women, and only one a scholar of colour.

As we highlight in later chapters, this is not just a case of tallying numbers: it is a significant omission to the development of robust understandings of social harm. As such, although we have given traction to some critiques in this chapter, I emphasise that it is worth men scholars in zemiology – and any other science – to reflect on what they are reading and, as such, what they are perhaps *not* reading when making significant claims around social science subjects.

and in order to expand the discipline to study a whole range of harms not captured by the criminal law. And within these efforts, a significant body of literature has emerged which encompasses a range of criminaliseable harms, from ethnic and religious intolerance to ecocide and genocide.

Indeed it should be noted that there are many examples of social harm approaches and criminological approaches overlapping. Take for example Steve Tombs' research on corporate crime. In acknowledging the harms people experience as a consequence of corporate deregulation and lack of legislation, Tombs argues for *increased* regulation and accountability when avoidable and foreseeable harms occur, often to the human cost of lower-level workers or working-class people (see Tombs, 2016; Tombs and Whyte, 2015). Tombs has pointed to the potential for developing a dual regulatory focus, both from a criminological and a zemiological perspective – for example, in relation to the lived realities of social harm in the context of the Grenfell Disaster of 2017 as outlined in the introductory chapter.

Similar approaches to regulation and criminalisation are taken by Jo Large, who evidences the harms of production and distribution in the 'fast-fashion' industry (cheap, affordable clothes often produced under exploitative conditions, with potential health harm consequences on those who produce them). Like Tombs, Large argues for improved regulation and enforcement so that companies, corporations and individuals can be held to account for harms and abuses that they perpetrate (Large, 2018). In practical senses, these arguments draw together social harm perspectives within the broader frame of critical criminology. That is to say, they aim to enact certain changes through law which could prevent future catastrophes or harms whilst enabling the criminalisation of responsible parties.

On the other hand, and as we will show in depth in Chapter 3, Victoria Canning uses the example of *border harms* as a means to specifically expand zemiological perspectives to understand the impacts of border controls on the lives of migrants. As we will see towards the end of this chapter, immigration is often conflated with 'crime' to the point that border-related discussions can become dominated by narratives of immigrant as 'criminal'. In 2006, Juliet Stumpf coined the term 'crimmigration' to highlight the extent of this phenomenon, and in particular the ways in which migrants are increasingly criminalised for migration-related offences rather than inherently harmful or violent acts. To this end, Canning has argued for a 'zemiology at the border' to move away from discourses of crime where immigration is concerned (see Canning, 2018). Although legislation has expanded to regulate the movement of people, many aspects of this are actually enacted outside of the realms of criminalisation or criminal 'justice' systems, and are instead through policy or civil sanctions (see Aliverti, 2012). Moreover, when we look more closely at the reality of border harms, we come to see that those most harmed by such processes are those who are often termed as 'illegal immigrants' themselves.

As we can see, there are many ways in which the subjects run parallel in interest and in outcomes. However, we argue that zemiology is a work in progress: its future projects may take on similar epistemological approaches, but the topics covered should move away from those defined as 'criminal' activities and focus solidly on significant, large-scale institutional harms. For an overview of similarities and divergences between the two approaches, see Table 2.2.

TABLE 2.2 Similarities and divergences in critical criminology and zemiology

Similarities	*Divergences*
Concern for documenting and addressing inequalities in society	Zemiology maintains primary focus on institutional, endemic and state-level endorsed harms. Critical criminology might otherwise focus on how these can be addressed from within criminology. In rejecting the elitist historical nature of language and definitions of crime and law, zemiology ideally focuses instead on harmful practices from outside of such structures and definitions. That is to say, it harbours more interest in the outcomes of unequal social processes which inflict harm.
Foundations in radical and critical thought	Both critical criminology and zemiology share similar epistemological foundations. Both are influenced to some degree by Marxian analyses of capitalism. Many thinkers in both fields also draw from feminism, critical race theory and abolitionist perspectives. For zemiologists, the issues raised by these groups – such as institutional and individual experiences of racism, classism, casteism or subjections to sexualised violence, should – where possible – be researched outside of systems of punishment and with the objective of facilitating structural change.
Dedication to social justice	Social justice can be defined in various ways, but fundamentally, those working towards social justice advocate positive change through processes of dismantlement or significant reform. Social justice should ideally lead to a redistribution of wealth, and create opportunities to equality in access (for example, to quality education). The term has been gradually co-opted into pro-capitalist agendas which drive individuals towards striving for equal access to wealth. For zemiologists – as with other critical and radical thinkers – this should be a restructuring of society, including dismantling cultural violence and inequalities, so that people may have opportunities to develop autonomy and collectively reduce socially harmful acts and institutional structures in society. For zemiologists, this should not be undertaken with agendas for reform if and when the original or ongoing agendas are set by those who are complicit in inflicting or perpetuating social harm on mass or industrial scales.

Conceptually within the vast terrain of critical criminological work, conduct norms, social aberrance, social deviance, social harm and social injury are just a few of the intellectual attempts to mark out a more inclusive set of harmful behaviours. Kramer (2013) provides a comprehensive overview of these attempts and argues that:

> international law in all of its forms can still provide a rhetorical touchstone for criminologists to frame judgments about what is and is not criminal. It can allow us to 'expand the core' of the discipline to better take into account corporate and state crimes.
>
> *(2013: 33)*

This is very similar to the stance taken by the Schwendingers (1970) but opposed by Green and Ward (2004) not only because many inequalities are widely accepted as legitimate but also because this conceptualisation breaks the link between crime and the notion of deviance.

Similarly, much critical criminology, for all of its significance, originality and sophistication, ends up in attempts to redefine the legitimate area of criminology and is based in an implicit or explicit call for law, not least criminal law, to be more effectively developed or enforced, in ways that promote greater social justice through criminal justice, and in ways that uphold or extend various rights.

In short, much of this work proceeds at least implicitly on the basis of a rights-based framework. But for us this is ultimately problematic, notwithstanding that some people may secure their basic rights through the criminal law and many more will buy into the notion of the possibility of justice, the majority of those affected by social harms will have little or no recognition by the formal system, particularly those victims of harms which are not captured by the criminal law. In other words, for many of the social harms upon which we and others have focused, law and rights are likely to be of very little relevance at all.

This is one of the key ways in which we can locate the relationships between critical criminology, social harm and zemiology. It is only the latter which essentially breaks from (actual or potential) legal definitions of harm, not least those linked to apparently progressive – but ultimately flawed (Fudge and Glasbeek, 1992) – rights-based frameworks. Thus, notwithstanding the need for its substance, contours and commitments to be much more fully developed, as indicated in the previous section, in recent years zemiology has increasingly been linked to some theory of human needs – a framework not linked to nor reliant upon law, jurisprudence or some other legal framework. Of particular significance here is the work of Pemberton (2007) and Pantazis and Pemberton (2009) who use Doyal and Gough's (1991) theory of human need to develop the concept of harm arguing that harm is perpetuated when specified needs are not fulfilled. Subsequently, Pemberton (2015) in *Harmful Societies* attempts to operationalise a needs approach to harm. He admits, however, at the outset that while much has been written about the potential of 'social harm', such an approach:

> remains a relatively empty space, insofar as few studies have actually sought to develop the conceptual lens and to operationalize it through empirical study. It is hoped that this book will contribute to how we may begin to collectively imagine an alternative approach to the study of harm.
>
> *(Pemberton, 2015: 11)*

He provides an excellent overview of the origins and debates around the concept of social harm both within and outside of criminology before analysing the performance of a number of selected states and regimes in relation to a range of harms. It is a highly original work, illustrating the potential as well as the pitfalls of a social harm approach. There is no doubt that he advances our understanding of social harm considerably, but has underscored the fact that a social harm approach is very much a work in progress (Tombs, 2015).

What is harm?

As we have noted, harm is absolutely not the sole preoccupation of any one discipline. Indeed, it is arguably the medical sciences which have the longest and most central such focus, specifically in the context of harm reduction where medical trials or behavioural risk assessments are prevalent (see Lesch *et al.*, 2009; Marlatt, 1996). However, in this section we expand our focus on harm in relation to the social sciences, focusing specifically on the differences between critical criminology, social harm and zemiology, considerations which pertain to the question of whether and how zemiology should be considered as a separate discipline or simply a branch of critical criminology, albeit the latter being one with a social-harm-approach twist.

Copson (2011) has analysed the fundamental differences which exist between the conceptualisations of harm within criminology, critical criminology and zemiology, reflecting different ideas and assumptions around issues of justice and liberty in the context of the fulfilment of human need. Criminology, she argues, deploys a liberal individualistic notion of harm as embraced by conventional jurisprudence. In contrast, zemiology situates harm in the context of human needs. Thus harm occurs when people are prevented by either the social structures or individual actions to meet their needs (see Tifft and Sullivan, 2001). Harm, in this sense, is linked to positive liberty in contrast to the negative liberties which law claims to protect and to which all forms of criminology are inevitably drawn. Critical criminology's notion of harm, she suggests, falls somewhere between the two positions. While increasingly recognising socially structured harm, nevertheless, it continues to embrace individualistic notions of harms articulated in rights or conventional jurisprudence. We shall explore related claims regarding the ontological basis of social harm further in Chapter 4.

On the distinction between social harm and zemiology, Pemberton has sought to provide some clarity:

> The existing literature confusingly makes reference to both social harm and zemiology, and at times these terms have been used interchangeably. For some, including myself, social harm represents the study of socially mediated harms, whereas zemiology, derived from the Greek *xemia* for harm, denotes the study of harm.
>
> *(Pemberton, 2015 :6)*

This is, he continues:

> more than an issue of semantics. Zemiology is preferable, insofar as a by-product of *Beyond criminology* has been the co-option of the language of social harm into criminological discourse ... Thus, zemiology would serve to demarcate those critical scholars whose interest lies 'beyond criminology' from criminologists using the notion of social harm, to establish an alternative field of study. Social harm therefore becomes the organising concept for zemiology as a field of study. When these distinctions are drawn, the emergent characteristics of zemiology can be more clearly articulated.
>
> *(Pemberton, 2015: 6–7)*

Thus he goes on to note five such emergent characteristics. First, following Hillyard and Tombs (2004), he notes that zemiology seeks "to provide an alternative lens that captures the vicissitudes of contemporary life" (Pemberton, 2015: 7). Second, it requires a shift in emphasis from individual level harms to those associated with states and corporations; third is a recognition that most widespread social harms "are not caused by intentional acts, but rather, result from the omission to act or societal indifference to suffering" (Pemberton, 2015: 8); and, fourth, that such harms are preventable, that is, products of social and economic organisation. This leads him, finally, to espouse for zemiology a reformist commitment to identifying "less harmful forms of capitalism" (Pemberton, 2015: 8).

This still begs the question, of course, of what is to be the basis for identifying a phenomenon as 'harmful' or a 'social harm', and thus falling within the legitimate ambit of zemiology?

'Knowing' social harm

It is clear, then, that there remains much work to be done in order to determine the ontological basis of a concept of social harm and, in turn, an object of study for zemiology – work to which we shall turn in the following two chapters. But prior to considering in detail how we might more effectively theorise what makes harm harmful, there is a different way of approaching this question; and here we would suggest that there is a great deal of agreement about certain phenomena being harmful. That we can make this statement about widespread agreement even in societies which are highly stratified through class, gendered, racialised cleavages is quite remarkable. Thus if we consider, for example, some forms of physical harms for which we have incidence data – 'Deaths Brought Forward' by air pollution, occupational deaths, and deaths as a result of food poisoning (Tombs and Whyte, 2015) – all of these seem to us to be incontestable *as harms*. The same observation could be made regarding excess winter deaths, discussed above. That is, most people in most places at most times would concur with labelling these phenomena as harmful. They would not necessarily agree which were more or less harmful, nor *how* harmful any of these harms are relative to other social harms, nor how any of these ranked in terms of harms to those harms proscribed by criminal law. But we would all agree these as harms. As we shall see in the next chapter, we can fairly easily go further than this – we can detail the dimensions of harms entailed in these different phenomena, how they harm, and say something about how they operate. The bottom line is that we might know much more about harm than some sceptics might concede!

In many respects, data on social harm is ubiquitous – it proliferates, is available on virtually every aspect of social life – and, therefore, on virtually any dimension of social harm. So we can access data on food poisoning in Ghana (Malm *et al.*, 2015), air pollution in India (The World Air Quality Index Project Team, n.d.), women's economic dependency in sub-Saharan Africa (United Nations, n.d.) or deaths of workers constructing infrastructure for the 2022 football World Cup in Qatar (Amnesty International, 2019). When Pemberton measured the extent of harm, he drew on (almost entirely) Organisation for Economic Co-operation and Development data sets across almost 20 areas of economic and social life, from trade union density to trust, pensions spend to prison rates (Pemberton, 2015: 67).

These points being made, we must, of course, recognise this data for what it is and treat it as critical social scientists. There are several (rather obvious) aspects to this observation.

First, supranational and national states bodies collect a mass of data, and this is generally accessible (and, where it is not immediately so, may be through national-specific freedom of information laws). But of course we use this as a raw material not as unproblematic indicators – we treat official data sceptically and interrogate and reconstruct this as feasible and appropriate (Tombs, 1990).

Second, we must also be cognisant of how and why data, especially state data, is gathered in the first place – and what definitions, categories and indeed motives might inform this. The controversies and complexities generated by the different bases upon which data is gathered – both inter- and intra-nationally – was well illustrated in claims and counterclaims regarding comparative death rates as a result of Covid-19 during the first half of 2020 (Richardson and Spiegelhalter, 2020).

Third, we must access supplementary data alongside that generated by state organisations. There is a mass of such data available. Of course, the above caveats about using state data apply here too – we cannot suspend our critical faculties whether our data is from liberal organisations such as the Business and Human Rights Resource Centre or Transparency International, or more politicised organisations such as, for example, the US-health and safety activist organisation (the National Council for Occupational Safety and Health) or Odhikar, a Dhaka-based human rights organisation.

These methodological points being made, if we can collate usable data on, say, fatal exposures to air pollution, to carcinogens in commercial or domestic use, to pesticides in food production and consumption, or lack of access to safe water, free basic education or maternity services, several conclusions can be drawn.

First, in each such area, which often fly below the academic radar, there are significant numbers of deaths, life-shortening and life-threatening illnesses. Moreover, as with all forms of physical harms, these harms are associated with a wider series of harms generated by each death, injury or illness. These might be financial, entailing a loss of income or additional costs incurred by the stricken person or his/her family members, or economic, in the sense of all of these harms entail various layers of costs for the state. Where the harms are generated in profit-making settings, these costs are socialised, while profits remain privatised – so there are harmful wealth-distribution effects, also. Moreover, associated with these harms are various emotional and psychological harms, many of which may be short-lived, others of which may endure over long periods.

Second, while statistics can be viewed as a collation of a series of isolated cases or incidents or harms, the harms captured in the above categories are much more usefully thought of not as incidents *per se*, but as processes, or effects of processes, indeed processes which arise in organisational settings, through forms of economic and social organisation, and in structures. So although these may *manifest* themselves at the level of individuals, they are not *explicable* at the level of individuals. Relatedly, effective responses to them cannot be achieved through systems of accountability developed on the basis of individual categories such as those upon which criminal law is based (see above).

Third, the reference to structures in the previous paragraph should highlight to us the fact that these and other forms of harms are not distributed randomly but highly differentially. In this respect it is often reasonable to emphasise the cumulative as opposed to the isolated experience of harm. This point is well made by Pemberton (2015), and developed in the following chapters. Moreover, the magnitude of these deaths is significantly greater than those deaths which are captured by the criminal law.

So, and in short, we believe that there is an awful lot to be said about social harm!

Beyond the individual

That said, what does it mean to call such harm *social*? The key achievement of the term 'social' in the couplet 'social harm' is to shift our level of explanation beyond the individual. We began the previous chapter by discussing the 'story of crime', with which we are all familiar, and which permeates popular, political and even academic consciousness. There is a further aspect to that story here, and this can be captured by the term 'proximity'. In many forms of harm upon which criminal justice systems overwhelmingly focus – crime – there is, or must at some point be, a degree of proximity between an offender and victim. This is most obviously the case with regard to personal assaults, robberies and so on. Yet, it also applies to non-contact theft and burglary, where the victims' 'space' is invaded for example, as an owner or a resident. By contrast, in the case of the kinds of harms which we have illustrated thus far, there are frequently enormous distances between the source and object of the harm, the 'offender' and 'victim', in terms of both space and time. So, for example, origins of the conditions which lead to excess winter deaths, or produce routine, large-scale food poisoning, worker deaths or environmental pollution are likely to involve collections of disparate individuals or groups of individuals engaged in actions, decisions or omissions separated from consequent deaths and illnesses in question by significant distance in terms of time and geography. These dimensions of lack of proximity run entirely contrary to our stories of crime – and also to the ways in which criminal law is constructed. Thus, distances of time and space make awareness of but certainly proving victimisation difficult if not impossible. Proximity, *mens rea*, and thus the possibilities of the kinds of accountability which the criminal justice system claims to be able to offer, are missing.

A focus on crime points us towards a focus on the inter-personal; by contrast, a social harm or zemiological approach leads us more inevitably, or at least more easily, both to understandings and to effective responses located beyond the level of individuals. That is, the term 'social' most notably says something about the origins and aetiology of harm – ultimately, as Pemberton (2015) clearly demonstrates, different forms of economic, political and social organisation produce different kinds and levels of harm. The focus on the social also reveals that those who experience harm do so not in a sporadic or random way – but systematically, so that harm tends to be experienced as a member of a social group, be this of minority status or relatively powerless or marginalised (Cain and Howe, 2008). So, for example, specific harms fall on women, people of colour, the homeless, the elderly, workers, and so on. Harm can also incorporate the individual impacts on people – families whose partner or parent die at work, or life course histories of harms which are compounded by structural conditions (Canning, 2017; Pantazis, 2008).

These harms are partly captured by the concept of 'structural violence' (Galtung, 1969) – but only partially so. The concept of structural violence is a useful one, directing our attention to outcomes and processes which cause harm and death, and which are avoidable, and all too often entail the state either facilitating or not alleviating such avoidable harms. But it needs supplementing with a meso-level concept of violence, namely institutional violence developed recently by Cooper and Whyte (2017).

Thus structural violence shifts:

> attention from action and intent to inaction, poor decision making and their subsequent consequences. Where there is capacity for people to live free from suffering, but no political will exists to implement change to alleviate such suffering, structural violence is present.
>
> *(Canning, 2017: 48)*

But it is not, as is frequently recognised, without its limitations (Tombs, 2018).

For one thing, structural violence is a very broad and all-encompassing concept. Perhaps this is one of its attractions – it defines as violence a whole range of harmful consequences which would otherwise be omitted from a more limited, 'dominant' understanding of violence. But this breadth can

BOX 2.2 STRUCTURAL VIOLENCE AND INSTITUTIONAL VIOLENCE

As Paul Farmer et al. outline, "*Structural violence*, a term coined by Johan Galtung and by liberation theologians during the 1960s, describes social structures – economic, political, legal, religious, and cultural – that stop individuals, groups, and societies from reaching their full potential. In its general usage, the word *violence* often conveys a physical image; however, according to Galtung, it is the 'avoidable impairment of fundamental human needs or … the impairment of human life, which lowers the actual degree to which someone is able to meet their needs below that which would otherwise be possible'. Structural violence is often embedded in longstanding 'ubiquitous social structures, normalized by stable institutions and regular experience'. Because they seem so ordinary in our ways of understanding the world, they appear almost invisible. Disparate access to resources, political power, education, health care, and legal standing are just a few examples. The idea of *structural violence* is linked very closely to *social injustice* and the social machinery of oppression" (2006).

This differs somewhat from *institutional violence* with which Cooper and Whyte (2017) seek to capture the relationships between "political violence and institutions that are tasked with implementing and administering key political objectives … This is a form of violence that can be understood as a means of force which is not simply acted upon, but organised and administered through *legitimate* means." For Cooper and Whyte, "'institutional violence' better describes the ordinary and mundane violence that make up lived experience of those subject to it – the lived experience of feeling humiliated, anxious and vilified. To talk about institutional violence means that we need to see violence not as 'exceptional' or 'unusual' events but 'ordinary' and 'mundane' processes that routinely and over time deteriorate our mental and physical health. Governments rely on the institutional machinery to translate economic reforms into policy and administer them in ways that achieve their main goals" (2017: 23–24).

be an advantage and a problem. Is violence simply the equivalent of harm? Where there are harmful consequences, has there always been or should we always be able to identify violence? These are difficult questions. It is certainly possible that as an all-encompassing concept, structural violence appears to include a vast range of phenomena which we can agree are harmful but perhaps are not necessarily violence. So perhaps there is greater accuracy in using the concept of social harm over structural violence.

Second, it is often very difficult to identify responsibility for such structural violence. If the source of structural violence is 'structures', what does it mean to say that? Does it mean we cannot identify responsibility for such violence – and, if so, how do we determine accountability, who or what should be called to account? And if we cannot call perpetrators to account, how can we minimise or prevent such violence from occurring? This is where Cooper and Whyte's reference to institutional violence is helpful, for it directs our attention to those bodies which implement political decisions, allowing us to identify concrete actions, inactions, working practices, cultures of organisations, and so on. So, for us, 'institutional violence' is a useful conceptual adjunct to structural violence (see Box 2.2).

However, a social harm approach has advantages over either or both. First, the determination of responsibility and accountability is intrinsic to the enterprise of social harm – albeit there is agreement within this perspective that accountability and responsibility will not be determined through criminal justice systems or criminal law. And, second, and to underline an obviousness, social harm foregrounds the social origins of harm and thus locates responsibility at the level of the social. This is not to exonerate individuals or specific institutions where responsibility accrues to them for any particular harm, but it is also to emphasise that it is difficult to think of any form of harm of any significance which does not have wider, social origins. And the logical corollary of this is that in identifying harms as social it is clear that the social origins of harm require a response at the level of the social – some form of organisation of the prevailing set of economic, political and/or social arrangements which have produced the harm.

Conclusion

As this chapter indicates, this book is far from the first to address the development of studies in social harm, nor to outline the sites of contestation between this and the origins of discussion in criminology. We have sought to follow these discussions and debates through since the inception of zemiology, specifically from the publication of *Beyond Criminology* and the subsequent critiques and developments.

Various critical criminologists have pointed to the fact that acts which are criminalised can also cause significant harm, and that this should not be undermined (see Hall and Winlow, 2018). Echoing some of the claims of the

Left Realists of the 1980s, crime should be taken seriously, they argue. Of course, we agree.

As individuals, we too are familiar with the harms of criminalised acts. Even since the inception of this very book, we have each been subject to various actions which fall under the category of 'crime'. Between us these included a house break-in and taking of cash, a hit and run car incident, personal theft, online fraud and a physical attack on a public street. By all accounts, these are fairly serious (and indeed unlucky for us!) experiences. As such, we are certainly not suggesting that such acts are not harmful or have not caused harm, nor that they would not have potential to lead to other harms, as outlined in the dimensions addressed in the previous chapter. A critical criminological project may consider why and how such violence exists, and how to reduce or respond to it usually within the confines of systems of punishment (although more progressive work has moved towards community restoration).

A zemiological perspective prefers to work outside of the realms of individualistic or street-level *crimes*. Although they can be harmful and indeed negatively impactful, as zemiologists we seek to consider socially and institutionalised harms which have far greater impacts on many more people. In sum, although we acknowledge the harms of some deviant or 'criminal' acts, we are more interested in training our focus on acts which often occur on grander scales and outside of the rule of law. Studying endemic harms requires us to 'look up' at powerful institutions, social structures and political elites.

The following chapters address how harm can be conceptualised. In Chapter 3, we set out an extended typology of harm – albeit one that remains provisional and subject to reflection and development. This, along with the subsequent chapter, Chapter 4, is one of two which seeks to determine in greater detail an adequate response to the question, what is social harm and what makes harm harmful? In any case, from here on in, determining what zemiology is and indeed how to 'do it' – rather than what it is not and from whence it emerged – becomes the central focus of this book.

References

Allen, G. and Kirk-Wade, E. (2020) *Terrorism in Great Britain: The Statistics*, London: House of Commons, https://commonslibrary.parliament.uk/research-briefings/cbp-7613/ (Accessed 7 July 2020).

Amnesty International (2019) *Migrants Rights with Four Years to the Qatar 2022 World Cup*, www.amnesty.org/en/latest/campaigns/2019/02/reality-check-migrant-workers-rights-with-four-years-to-qatar-2022-world-cup/ (Accessed 13 October 2020).

Boukli, P. and Kotzé, J. (2018) Introduction, in *Zemiology: Reconnecting Crime and Social Harm*, edited by P. Boukli and J. Kotzé, Basingstoke: Palgrave Macmillan, 1–11.

Brogden, M. and Nijhar, P. (2006) Crime, abuse and social harm: Towards an integrated approach, in *Aging, Crime and Society*, edited by A. Wahidin and M. Cain, London: Routledge, 35–52.

Cain, M. and Howe, A. (2008) *Women, Crime and Social Harm: Towards a Criminology for the Global Era*, Portland: Hart Publishing.

Canning, V. (2017) *Gendered Harm and Structural Violence in the British Asylum System*, Oxon: Routledge.

Canning, V. (2018) Zemiology at the border, in *Zemiology: Reconnecting Crime and Social Harm*, edited by P. Boukli and J. Kotzé, Basingstoke: Palgrave Macmillan, 183–103.

Carroll, L. (1934) *Through the Looking-Glass*, first published in 1872.

Cooper, V. and Whyte, D., eds. (2017) *The Violence of Austerity*, London: Pluto Press.

Copson, Lynne (2011) *Archaeologies of Harm: Criminology, Critical Criminology, Zemiology*. Unpublished PhD Thesis, Faculty of Social Sciences and Law, School of Sociology, University of Bristol.

Davies, P., Francis, P. and Wyatt, T., eds. (2014) *Invisible Crimes and Social Harms*, Basingstoke: Palgrave Macmillan.

Doyal, L. and Gough, I. (1991) *A Theory of Human Need*, Basingstoke: Palgrave Macmillan.

Farmer, P. E., Nizeye, B., Stulac, S. and Keshavjee, S. (2006) Structural violence and clinical medicine, *PLoS Medicine*, 3 (10), e449, https://doi.org/10.1371/journal.pmed.0030449 (Accessed 10 June 2020).

Feeley, M. (2014) *Learning Care Lessons: Literacy, Love, Care and Solidarity*, London: The Tufnell Press.

Foucault, M. (1977) *Discipline and Punish*, London: Allen Lane.

Foucault, M. (1979) *The History of Sexuality, Vol. 1: An Introduction*, London: Allen Lane, Penguin Press.

Freudenberg, N. (2014) *Lethal but Legal: Corporations, Consumption, and Protecting Public Health*, Oxford: Oxford University Press.

Fudge, J. and Glasbeek, H. (1992) The politics of rights: A politics with little class, *Social & Legal Studies*, 1, 45–70.

Galtung, J. (1969) Violence, peace, and peace research, *Journal of Peace Research*, 6 (3), 167–191.

Green, P. and Ward, T. (2004) *State Crime: Governments, Violence and Corruption*, London: Pluto Press.

Guertler, P. and Smith, P. (2018) *Cold Homes and Excess Winter Deaths: A Preventable Public Health Epidemic That Can No Longer Be Tolerated*, E3G Briefing Paper, February 2018, www.nea.org.uk/wp-content/uploads/2018/02/E3G-NEA-Cold-homes-and-excess-winter-deaths.pdf (Accessed 10 June 2020).

Hall, S. and Winlow, S. (2018) Big trouble or little evils: The ideological struggle over the concept of harm, in *Zemiology: Reconnecting Crime and Social Harm*, edited by A. Boukli and J. Kotzé, Switzerland: Palgrave Macmillan, 107–126.

Hillyard, P. and Tombs, S. (2004) Beyond criminology?, in *Beyond Criminology: Taking Harm Seriously*, edited by P. Hillyard, C. Pantazis, S. Tombs and D. Gordon, London: Pluto Press, 10–29.

Hillyard, P. and Tombs, S. (2017) Social harm and zemiology, in *The Oxford Handbook of Criminology*, edited by A. Liebling, S. Maruna and L. McAra, Oxford: Oxford University Press, 284–305.

Hillyard, P., C. Pantazis, S. Tombs and D. Gordon, eds. (2004) *Beyond Criminology: Taking Harm Seriously*, London: Pluto.

Hope, A. (2013) The shackled school internet: Zemiological solutions to the problem of over-blocking, *Learning, Media and Technology*, 38, 270–281.

Hughes, G. (2007) *The Politics of Crime and Community*, London: Palgrave Macmillan.

Kramer, R. C. (2013) *Expanding the Core: Blameworthy Harms, International Law and State-Corporate Crimes*, Paper presented at the Presidential Panel, 'Reconsidering the Legal Definition of Crime' at the annual meeting of the American Society of Criminology, 21 November 2013, Atlanta.

Large, J. (2018) Spot the fashion victim(s): The importance of rethinking harm within the context of fashion counterfeiting, in *Zemiology: Reconnecting Crime and Social Harm*, edited by A. Boukli and J. Kotze, Switzerland: Palgrave Macmillan, 223–245.

Lesch, A., Kafaar, Z. and Kagee, A. (2009) Participation in HIV vaccine trials, in *HIV/AIDS in South Africa 25 Years On*, edited by P. Rohleder, L. Swartz, S. Kalichman and Leickness S., New York: Springer, 337–351.

Lloyd, A. (2018) *The Harms of Work*, Bristol: Policy Press.

Loader, I. and Sparks, R. (2011) *Public Criminology?* London: Routledge.

Machniewski, S. (2010) *Social Harm and Older People in Northern Ireland*, dissertation submitted to Queen's University Belfast in accordance with the requirements for the award of the degree of Doctor of Philosophy in the Faculty of Arts, Humanities and Social Sciences.

Malm, K. L., Nyarko, K. M., Yawson, A. E., Gogo, B., Lawson, A. and Afari, E. (2015) Foodborne illness among school children in Ga East, Accra, *Ghana Medical Journal*, 49 (2), 72–76.

Marlatt, A. (1996) Harm reduction: Come as you are, *Addictive Behaviors*, 21 (6), 779–778.

Maruna, S. (2013) *Expert Witness for the Defence in the Mock Trial of Criminology*, Wolverhampton: British Society of Criminology.

McGill, C. H. (2012) The hidden environmental harms of the cut-flower industry, *Neo: A Journal of Student Research*, 2 (1), http://eprints.lincoln.ac.uk/16180/ (Accessed 14 August 2020).

McLaughlin, E. and Muncie, J. (2013) *The SAGE Dictionary of Criminology*, 3rd ed., London: Sage.

Mitchell, D., Pantazis, C. and Pemberton, S., eds. (2019) Neo-liberalism and harm production, Special Issue of *Justice, Power and Resistance*, 3 (2).

Muncie, J. (2005) Book review of *Beyond Criminology: Taking Harm Seriously*, *Crime, Law and Social Change*, 43.

Muncie, J. (2013) Social harm, in *The Sage Dictionary of Criminology*, 3rd ed., edited by E. McLaughlin and J. Muncie, London: Sage, 430–432.
Office for National Statistics (2019) *Excess Winter Mortality in England and Wales: 2018 to 2019 (Provisional) and 2017 to 2018 (Final)*, 27 November, www.ons.gov.uk/peoplepopulationandcommunity/birthsdeathsandmarriages/deaths/bulletins/excesswintermortalityinenglandandwales/2018to2019provisionaland2017to2018final (Accessed 14 August 2020).
Pantazis, C. (2008) The problem with criminalisation, *Criminal Justice Matters*, 74 (1), 10–12.
Pantazis, C. and Pemberton, S. (2009) Nation states and the production of social harm: Resisting the hegemony of 'TINA', in *State, Crime, Power*, edited by R. Coleman, J. Sim, S. Tombs and D. Whyte, London: Sage, 214–233.
Pantazis, C., Pemberton, S. and Mitchell, D., eds. (2019) Culture, consumption and social harm. Special Issue of *Justice, Power and Resistance*, 3 (2).
Passas, N. and Goodwin, N. R., eds. (2004) *It's Legal but It Ain't Right: Harmful Social Consequences of Legal Industries*, Michigan: University of Michigan Press.
Pavlich, G. (1999) Criticism and criminology: In search of legitimacy, *Theoretical Criminology*, 3, 136–152.
Pemberton, S. (2007) Social harm future(s): Exploring the potential of the social harm approach, *Crime, Law and Social Change*, 48, 27–41.
Pemberton, S. (2015) *Harmful Societies: Understanding Social Harm*, Bristol: Policy Press.
Phillips, J. (2007) *Care*, London: Polity.
Presser, L. (2013) *Why We Harm*, New Brunswick, NJ: Rutgers University Press.
Reiman, J. (2006) Book review of *Beyond Criminology: Taking Harm Seriously*, *British Journal of Criminology*, 46, 362–364.
Richardson, S. and Spiegelhalter, D. (2020) Coronavirus statistics: What can we trust and what should we ignore?, *The Observer*, 12 April.
Schwendinger, H. and Schwendinger, J. (1970) Defenders of order or guardians of human rights?, *Issues in Criminology*, 5, 123–157.
Scott, S. (2017) *Labour Exploitation and Work-Based Harm*, Bristol: Policy Press.
Smart, C. (1990) Feminist approaches to criminology, or postmodern woman meets atavistic man, in *Feminist Perspectives in Criminology*, edited by L. Gelsthorpe and A. Morris, Milton Keynes: Open University Press, 70–84.
The World Air Quality Index Project Team (n.d.) *Air Pollution in India: Real-Time Air Quality Index Visual Map*, https://aqicn.org/map/india/ (Accessed 14 August 2020).
Tifft, L. and Sullivan, D. C. (2001) A needs based social harm definition of crime, in *What Is Crime? Controversies over the Nature of Crime and What to Do About It*, edited by S. Henry and M. Lanier, Lanham, MD: Rowman & Littlefield, 179–203.
Tombs, S. (1990) Industrial injuries in British manufacturing, *Sociological Review*, 38, (2), 324–343.
Tombs, S. (2015) Harmful societies, *Criminal Justice Matters*, 101, 36–37.
Tombs, S. (2016) *Social Protection After the Crisis: Regulation Without Enforcement*, Bristol: Policy Press.
Tombs, S. (2018) Structural violence, in *Criminological Theories and Concepts*, edited by V. Cooper and J. Phoenix, Milton Keynes: The Open University, 243–272.

Tombs, S. and Whyte, D., eds. (2003) *Unmasking the Crimes of the Powerful: Scrutinising States and Corporations*, New York/London: Peter Lang.
Tombs, S. and Whyte, D. (2015) *The Corporate Criminal: Why Corporations Must Be Abolished*, Oxon: Routledge.
United Nations (n.d.) *The World's Women 2015*, https://unstats.un.org/unsd/gender/chapter8/chapter8.html (Accessed 14 August 2020).
Walters, R. (2003) *Deviant Knowledge: Criminology, Politics and Policy*, London: Taylor & Francis.
White, R. (2014) *Environmental Harm: An Eco-justice Perspective*, Bristol: Policy Press.

3
A PROVISIONAL TYPOLOGY OF HARM

Introduction

Thus far this book has considered the development of a social harm approach in relation to criminology in general and to critical criminology in particular. That said, harm itself is studied on much broader bases which are not confined to criminology, such as harms in the workplace (Lloyd, 2018; Presser, 2014), gendered harms (Cain and Howe, 2008), self-harm (Laye-Gindhu and Schonert-Reichl, 2005) and harm as a matter of risk (ESRC, 2013). Moreover, there has been an interesting move amongst various anthropologists and zemiologists to develop an anthropological zemiology as a means to situate harm and social suffering as a divergent field of analysis and action.[1] Likewise, harm has significant traction *outside* of the social sciences, notably in medical sciences where harm avoidance, reduction and mitigation are ostensibly the informing rationales of thought and practice. The potential for human risk is calculated to avoid the potential for medical harms. In this chapter we begin to elaborate the variety of meanings of social harm, exploring types, and some key characteristics, of harm.

What sets zemiological discussions of social harm aside from this broader base is its starting point in and subsequent rejection of normative definitions of 'crime'. As we have seen to this point, and will again discuss in Chapter 4, whilst some criminological studies focus on harms in relation to crime, zemiology aims to move away from crime narratives altogether. This is not to say that acts which are deemed to be crimes or criminal are not important or indeed harmful, but that a zemiological approach should emphasise and focus

FIGURE 3.1 From criminology to zemiology

on those acts or omissions which are more likely to cause us significant harm under the dimension of harms highlighted here – but more significantly must focus upon conditions, states of affairs, structures and processes including, of course, processes of criminalisation.

A move towards zemiology (see Figure 3.1) should not be construed as entirely disregarding the problematic – and considerable achievements – of *critical* criminology. Although earlier discussions amongst those working to develop a social harm perspective levelled significant criticism at criminology as a whole, there are parallels between *critical* or *radical* criminology and zemiology. As Zedner points out, harm is itself central to many aspects of criminology: those affected by violent crimes, for example, can experience significant harm (2011). Copson notes that "these perspectives risk either becoming polarised into competing subjects or harmonised to the point that issues of social harm are simply co-opted into the *raison d'être of criminology*" (2018: 34). While we are clear that zemiology is distinct from, and not a sub-genre within, critical criminology, it is equally clear to us that these enterprises are not diametrically opposed nor essentially antagonistic, but indeed share certain commitments and tendencies.

A typology of harm?

If we are to clearly depart the terrain of criminology then we need to clarify our object of focus: harm. Outlining forms of harm is a useful way to establish what is meant by *harm*, and indeed in gauging or deciding ways to measure it. This is one issue that has received criticism in the study of social harm: if crime has no ontological reality, then how can harm? Likewise, if we begin to separate out forms of harm then perhaps there is a danger in creating hierarchies of harm, and as such risk losing a structural focus on social inequalities which lead to or exacerbate certain harms. Lasslett in particular has pointed out this limitation by highlighting that harm and injustice have the potential to become conflated (Lasslett, 2010: 13).

In seeking to mark out the terrain constituted by 'social harm', Hillyard and Tombs (2004) had originally suggested a fourfold typology, some elements of which, if not wholly unproblematic, are in essence at least more self-evident than others. This typology incorporated: physical harms; financial/economic harms, the former located at the level of individuals and households, the latter at the local, regional or national levels; emotional and psychological harm; and harms arising out of a denial of what Alvesalo (1999: 4) had termed 'cultural safety', encompassing notions of autonomy, development and growth, and access to cultural, intellectual and information resources generally available in any given society. Subsequently, while there was very little discussion about these categories *per se*, much of the critical reaction to Hillyard, Tombs and others' work involved a critique of questioning the ontological basis of social harm (see, for example, Garside, 2013 and Lasslett, 2010). In one such consideration, Majid Yar claimed misrecognition as the ontological basis for social harm (Yar, 2012). While Tombs has argued that he finds this claim in itself unconvincing (Tombs, 2018), it does seem to us wholly persuasive to see misrecognition as a key *dimension* of social harm, one capturing a relational lack of respect for human dignity, integrity and wellbeing – which, as we note below, in its extreme form might be captured by the term 'contempt'.

In what remains the most developed single treatment of social harm, Pemberton (2015) sets out an over-lapping but distinct typology of harms, which incorporates: physical and mental health harms; autonomy harms, which result from situations where we experience 'fundamental disablement' in relation to our attempts to achieve self-actualisation; and relational harms, the latter coming in two forms – harms resulting from enforced exclusion from social relationships (enforced exclusion from personal relationships and social networks) and harms of misrecognition, which result from the symbolic injuries which serve to misrepresent the identities of individuals belonging to specific social groups (Pemberton, 2015: 13–34).

In what follows, we draw upon the above work to set out a provisional typology of harms, and we will address the following:

- physical harms;
- emotional and psychological harms, which capture Pemberton's 'mental health harms';
- financial and economic harms, which were set out in Hillyard and Tombs' original (2004) formulation, albeit we distinguish here slightly between these;

- cultural harms, encompassing some aspects of Alvesalo's 'cultural safety' but drawing upon a recent, extensive, potentially very significant consideration by Boukli and Copson (2020) and Copson (2018);
- harms of recognition, which raises to the fore one aspect of Pemberton's 'relational harm', although we discuss the latter as a separate category;
- autonomy harms, as set out by Pemberton (2015), albeit these are very close to 'harms of recognition'.

Some prior points.

First, as both the question mark in the title of this section indicates and as is noted in the bullet point list, this typology is provisional and thus intended to generate rather than close down discussion – and will be further revised and refined, as we note below. For example, even in setting these out we are aware that some categories could be collapsed into others, others more clearly extended.

Second, the types or categories of harm deployed below are heuristic, a combination of the descriptive and the analytical – thus, in the real world, there is overlap, and indeed what are presented as apparently discrete harms in fact impact in combination and do so differentially upon specific groups of people, thus multiplying the harms they produce; the harms and their impacts are layered and synergistic.

Third, then, while this might appear a simple 'typology' of harms, in fact these dimensions of harm need to be understood complexly: they have numerous dimensions, some of which are much more readily apparent than others; and they unfold in ripples, dispersing geographically and longitudinally.

Finally, if this schema of various dimensions of harm is provisional then it is, crucially, to be further developed and refined through the reflections of individuals, households and communities upon harms they experience beyond those captured by these dimensions. Indeed, this is a form of praxis which Hillyard and Tombs had originally claimed as one of the progressive elements of a social harm approach, that is, that it was informed by active citizens and not imposed upon them by academics under claims of objectivity or scientificity. This fluidity of 'harm' is a point to which we shall return, since it has implications for any discussion of the ontology of harm.

Physical harms

Physical harms are often construed as the easiest to define or measure: death, illness and injury are the obvious forms. These may develop from various avoidable social scenarios, for example through torture, sexual abuse or homicide. These examples fit quite easily within realms of criminal accountability, that is that there is a perpetrator who can be identified (although this is often complex in the case of state violence and torture; see Green and Ward, 2004 and Rejali, 2007).

However, not all physical harms are forms of direct physical violence. As we saw with Grenfell, multiple fatality incidents – notably in workplaces, transport, leisure or housing settings – are hardly uncommon and often easily preventable. These often achieve significant international resonance – Bhopal (see Box 3.1), Chernobyl, Minamata and Rana Plaza are obvious examples here. The preventable nature of many so-called 'natural disasters' also raises the toll of deaths from physical harms – tsunamis, pandemics, earthquakes, hurricanes and fires can all lead to more or less deaths dependent upon the extent to which states invest in prevention and mitigation for their populations.

People die prematurely – if more routinely, mundanely and beneath the radar – in many other ways, for example, in car accidents or house fires, from food poisoning or errors by doctors or surgeons. They may die from air pollution or from water which is chemically polluted. A key observation, however, is that, while at an individual level such deaths may be experienced and understood as atomised, unavoidable tragedies, when viewed socially it is clear that most forms of death can be more or less prevented.

Some deaths are easily preventable. It is widely estimated that about 10 million children die across the world each year – and about two thirds of these, some 6 million, die from water-related illnesses such as campylobacter, giardia and salmonella. In principle, these deaths are easily preventable, with the solutions being fundamentally in water and sanitation or, as David Roberts states, "Put very briefly and very simply, it is a case of 'clean water in, dirty water out'" (Roberts, 2009: 3).

Slightly more complexly, in 2020, the World Health Organization reported that tobacco kills more 8 million people each year as a result of direct use and indirect exposure. Moreover, "over 80% of the world's 1.3 billion tobacco users live in low- and middle-income countries" (WHO, 2020). Even just a slightly more cursory examination of the data on trends in deaths from tobacco amplifies that last remark about low- and middle-income countries. Thus, examining worldwide trends in deaths from smoking from 1990–2017:

> What we find is that the total number of deaths attributed to smoking are falling in many rich countries today … [A]cross Western Europe, the United States and Canada … more people were dying as a result of smoking a few decades ago versus today.
>
> The opposite is true for most low and middle income countries today. Although death rates from smoking tend to be falling, population

BOX 3.1 PHYSICAL HARM CASE STUDY: MASS POISONING IN BHOPAL

In June 2010, over 25 years after the massive gas leak which killed thousands at a chemical plant in Bhopal, Madhya Pradesh, an Indian court finally handed down sentences following successful criminal prosecutions related to the disaster. After the original charges of culpable homicide had been watered down, seven senior managers working at the Bhopal plant in 1984 were found guilty of death by neglect (an eighth so charged had died during the legal process), given two-year prison sentences and fined the equivalent of approximately $2,100. Union Carbide India Ltd (UCIL), then a subsidiary of the American company Union Carbide Corporation (UCC) and since 1995 of Eveready Industries India Ltd (EIIL), was fined $11,000. All those found guilty were Indian nationals but Warren Anderson, American CEO of UCC at the time of the gas leak, UCC itself and Union Carbide Eastern (UCE), another subsidiary of UCC with oversight over UCIL, could not be considered for trial in their absence: the court labelled these three named defendants 'absconders'.

Over 25 years earlier, in the morning of December 3 1984, the Union Carbide chemical plant had begun to spew out a cocktail of gases, vapours and liquids, forming a large low-lying cloud which spread out from the plant. Local people had no way of knowing how to prepare for or respond to any gas leak. They had never been told about the toxicity of the chemicals used by the company.

The gas which had leaked was the highly toxic methylisocyanate (MIC). Union Carbide Corporation had originally intended to locate the factory using the MIC process in France – but French unions successfully resisted the use of such a toxic production process. In keeping with the 'export of hazard', the US-owned multinational then decided to relocate the plant and its deadly technology to less-regulated India.

Estimates of how many were affected immediately and in the longer term by the gas cloud vary considerably. Initially the Indian Government stated that there had been 1,700 immediate deaths, a figure subsequently revised upwards to 3,329. In 2004, an Amnesty International report marking the 20th anniversary of the disaster claimed a minimum of 7,000 immediate deaths, a subsequent 15,000, with 100,000 'survivors' unable to work again (Amnesty International,

2004). The Sambhavna clinic, established in Bhopal to treat the gas victims, has estimated that, "Half a million people were exposed to the gas and 25,000 have died to date as a result of their exposure. More than 120,000 people still suffer from ailments caused by the accident and the subsequent pollution at the plant site" (The Bhopal Medical Appeal, n.d.).

The disaster at the plant – where many safety systems were inoperative and had been allowed to run down, with maintenance work cancelled as the plant had been deemed unprofitable by its US parent – was one of almost unimaginable proportions and with long-lasting and lingering negative effects. Various chemicals known to cause cancer, birth defects and brain damage continue to be found in local groundwater and wells (The Bhopal Medical Appeal, n.d.). These have never been subject to any sustained 'clean up' operation. Although assuming the assets and liabilities of UCC in a hostile merger in 2001, Dow Chemical Corporation has consistently refused to accept responsibility for the clean-up of the Bhopal area, where groundwater remains highly contaminated.

Pearce and Tombs (2012)

growth and ageing in these countries means the total number of deaths has continued to increase in recent decades.

(Ritchie and Roser, 2019)

The decreases in deaths from tobacco use show clearly that these types of deaths are preventable through a range of actions: legal and regulatory, prohibiting where and how tobacco can be bought, advertised and used; financial, through raising the costs of tobacco products; and cultural, by making tobacco use ever less socially acceptable. At the same time, these tend to be nationally based initiatives and certainly the global trends need to take into account the abilities of a global industry to redirect marketing, distribution and sales efforts from more to less regulated contexts, a specific manifestation of a phenomenon known as the export of hazard (Castleman, 1979; Ives, 1985).

Physical harms span significant terrain. They are the outcome of lack of adequate food or shelter. They may be related to car accidents, workplace hazards or illness through pollution. As the tobacco example indicates, their prevalence needs to be related to the wider socio-political environments within which we live, and where many harmful activities, conditions and processes either go unregulated or are normalised, accepted, even promoted. Thus Pemberton had outlined a variety of physical harms, including: long-term physical health problems; disease; malnutrition; illness; death; mental health problems. He noted that these may be linked to:

- generally poor quality of life;
- little or no access to a healthy diet;
- little or no opportunity to exercise effectively;
- poor access to appropriate health care;
- inadequate shelter and/or hazardous working or living environments.

Emotional and psychological harms

Emotional and psychological harms often develop from traumatic instances at one end (such as witnessing death or violence), or ongoing mental and emotional distress related to everyday pressures or problems (such as poverty) on the other. These are distinct phenomena, since one requires psychological diagnosis and possibly even intervention, whilst the other – emotional harm – is broader but still strongly related.

Hillyard and Tombs argued that emotional and psychological harms are "much more difficult to measure and relate to specific causes" (2004: 20). Physical injury or death can often be seen and usually easily identified, but feminist and psychological literatures have provided many examples which indicate otherwise in the cases of emotional and psychological harms. This is particularly the case for work which evidences the emotional and psychological harms that result from torture, sexual violence and domestic abuse (Arcel, 2003; Boyle, 2017; Canning, 2016, 2017; Dehghan, 2018; Herman, 1992; Jones and Cook, 2008).

Although individuals may each respond to harm in different ways, the spectrum of emotional and psychological harms is vast and, on the contrary, can often be identified and understood if appropriately explored. For example, problems such as sleeplessness, anxiety, depression or suicidality can be the outcome of instances of violence or other traumata. What lies at the source of the problem of measuring or relating to specific causes is the lack of capacity or space for these to be drawn out. To relate to specific causes, one must be provided with the ability to speak to the causes (Herman, 1992). However, those violences which cause most emotional harm – such as sexual violence, domestic terror or torture – remain socially silenced in a multitude of ways.

Pemberton (2015) collapsed these to refer to mental health harms in a variety of manifestations, including depression, anxiety, self-harm, suicidality, anxiety, variable phobias, symptoms attributed to Post-Traumatic Stress Disorder. He attributed these to various conditions, including the following:

- poor quality of life, loneliness, isolation;
- being subjected to abuse or violence which negatively impacts mental health and wellbeing;
- compounded by social issues such as insecurity, homelessness, poverty and destitution, poor or exploitative working conditions.

If psychological and emotional traumas appear individualised, or manifest themselves at the level of individuals, they can of course be discerned across communities and societies. The very idea of 'terrorism', of course, is predicated in creating emotional uncertainly for populations; the widespread reality of sexual violence impacts upon most women in most societies at some points; and in the wake of the resurgence of the Black Lives Matter movement following the killing of George Floyd, many black parents discussed 'the talk' they have to have with their children to warn them of the realities of discrimination from authority figures in general and the police in particular – thereby both underscoring but providing tools to deal with the emotional trauma to which people of colour are exposed in the face of white privilege on a daily basis (McDonald, 2020).

Somewhat differently, on a quite distinct scale, but, one suspects, of ubiquitous relevance, a recent study of the effects of the early stages of fracking (unconventional gas and oil extraction) in Lancashire analyses the relationships between fracking, social harm and 'collective trauma' on the part of affected communities (Short and Szolucha, 2017). Undertaking a social and environmental impact study upon citizens, they highlight a series of social harms that occurred at the planning, approval and exploration stages for fracking amounting to a 'collective trauma' being experienced by these rural communities. They document the traumatic experiences of local residents caused by a combination of factors and practices, including: truck traffic; local industrialisation; water pollution; air quality; noise; and fears for increasing, unpredictable and dangerous seismic activity. They then document a panoply of neo-liberal, pro-fracking business-friendly legal, regulatory and political pressures which bear down on the residents to seek to quell their objections and dismiss their concerns. Overall, they state that this unfolding "situation will have significant and long-lasting impacts on the local community, contributing to the collective trauma already experienced by the residents living in the vicinity of potential fracking sites in Lancashire" (Short and Szolucha, 2017: 274).

Financial and economic harms

Collapsed into this category or type of social harms are the following:

- Financial harms, that is monetary harms which affect individuals or households. These may be temporary, such as loss through theft or fraud, or an immediate loss of income due to, for example, unemployment; or they may be much longer term, as a result of no or precarious employment, high rental and livings costs, or lack of affordable access to basic amenities of life such as education, health care, transportation and so on.
- Economic harms are also monetary harms but affecting wider communities, or significant portions of them, and, in a global sense, whole societies and nation states.

'Financial' and 'economic' likely point to distinct levels of monetary harm, but it might be argued that their origins, the factors which maintain them, and their various effects, are so similar that they can be collapsed into one type.

In a general sense, financial harms have been discussed by those interested in social harm in relation to poverty – an extended concern for Pemberton (2015), for example. And when seen from a social point of view, and aside from ideological understandings of poverty in terms of poor life-decision and individual choice, then poverty is an outcome of uneven or unfair distributions of wealth. And so then, at a macro level, many foreseeable socio-economic decisions facilitate the ongoing existence of poverty: countries or states which charge for primary health care; reductions in trade and local industries; decreases in welfare entitlements; the list goes on. On the other side of this coin is, for example, tax breaks or tax havens for richer people which could otherwise facilitate wealth redistribution and tackle poverty. These often work within the law, and yet poverty has devastating economic harms which can result in physical harm, emotional and psychological harm and even death.

More broadly, financial and economic harms might emanate from misappropriation of funds by governments, malpractice by private corporations and private individuals, increased prices through cartelisation and price-fixing, and redistribution of wealth and income from the poorer to the richer through regressive taxation and welfare policies. Financial and economic harm can therefore also incorporate wider social harms, including the mental or emotional effects of job or property loss, and the relational harms which families or social units living together can experience when financial pressures push them apart.

In some instances, financial/economic harms and their consequences may relate to structural violence. That is to say that where harms are experienced by any given population or demographic which could otherwise be avoided by redistribution, and in particular if they are foreseeable, then structures in society are responsible for inflicting violence (Galtung, 1969). In other instances, where financial decisions are made through, for example, corporations or local councils and which inflict or fail to avoid foreseeable harms, then institutional violence can be present (see Cooper and Whyte, 2017b). These might include, though are not limited to, risky banking or corporate investment of public funds which could be spent elsewhere, or which may have foreseeable and long-term implications for those most dependent on welfare or support.

This was very much the case with the implementation of austerity measures in the aftermath of the Global Financial Crisis of 2007–2008, which lead to a worldwide economic recession and the deaths of hundreds of thousands of people through welfare cuts and healthcare reductions (Dorling, 2019). Whilst 36 bankers were famously imprisoned in Iceland for their role in facilitating financial harms through the misadventures of the banking system, most other countries moved towards increased taxation of citizens and reductions in public spending. Writing as Governments across the globe are counting the economic cost of coronavirus, it is hardly inconceivable that new waves of austerity are about to be unleashed on diverse populations – with diverse, disastrous and long-term effects (Cooper and Whyte, 2017a).

As Box 3.2 also demonstrates, financial and economic harms may also be the by-product of wider politicised decisions, such as in the case of the Occupation of Iraq.

Cultural harms

Pemberton's (2015) category of 'relational harms' had identified as one form of the latter a type of 'forced exclusion' which includes lack of social networks due to, for example, a lack of access to childcare and a physical and social isolation. Further, Alvesalo (1999: 4) had argued earlier that a developed understanding of social harm could include reference to 'cultural safety', encompassing access to cultural, intellectual and informational resources generally available in any given society.

Boukli and Copson (2020) subsequently set out three ways in which 'cultural harm' had been implicitly defined, based upon a review of literature around 'cultural harm', which they summarise thus: cultural harm as harm *to* culture; cultural harm as harm *by* culture; and cultural harm as misrecognition (Boukli and Copson, 2020: 32).

BOX 3.2 FINANCIAL AND ECONOMIC HARM CASE STUDY: NEO-LIBERALISM AND THE OCCUPATION OF IRAQ

In 2003, a United States-led alliance between the United Kingdom, Australia and Poland invaded Iraq – a country erroneously declared to be developing and harbouring 'weapons of mass destruction'. The invasion itself lasted more than a month, although conflict would continue, and led to what would be determined as an illegal occupation of Iraq.

The political motives for the occupation were highlighted as state crimes by criminologists (Green and Ward, 2004; Whyte, 2007). Indeed, Whyte demonstrated that a key underlying motive for the occupation – the appropriation of Iraq's oil industry – was as a case of corporate criminality. Fraud, embezzlement, deception and money laundering were rife. However, as Whyte would later go on to address, immunity and a lack of criminal accountability continued – even after an in-depth inquiry (Chilcot, 2016). Although international laws prohibit the forced economic transformation of an occupied country, the US-UK alliance had done just that. Oil and revenue were extracted, and previously untouchable agricultural stock (such as lamb and sheep) were forcibly made available for international trade. Those accountable for the occupation, namely former US president George Bush Junior and former UK prime minister Tony Blair, have never faced criminal sanctions or prosecution (Muttitt and Whyte, 2016).

This thus brings us to consider the longer-term harms of an arguably violent economic decision. Enforced through war-making (Ruggiero, 2016), neo-liberal trade routes were opened and Iraq's already hindered economy suffered immensely. In the aftermath of occupation, the unemployment rate rose from around 30 percent to 60 percent (Global Policy Forum, 2011). Whilst the physical harms of war are evidenced in the numbers of civilian deaths (exceeding 180,000), the economic harms were deeply impactful in various ways. As the Watson Institute of International and Public Affairs and Brown University noted (2018), "several times as many Iraqi civilians may have died as an indirect result of the war, due to damage to the systems that provide food, health care and clean drinking water, and as a result, illness, infectious diseases, and malnutrition that could otherwise have been avoided or treated", and thus economic harms continued to contribute to a continuum of social harms.

Cultural harm as harm *to* culture is, they state, following Tombs (2019), "harm that arises through the destruction or undermining of particular cultures or ways of being" or, as he added, accustomed modes of living and being (see Box 3.3). This harm can result from "acts such as the destruction or misuse of cultural artefacts or, more subtly, through the undermining of particular communities" (Boukli and Copson, 2020: 32).

Cultural harm as harm *by* culture refers to harms that result from the imposition of a particular culture: "This can either be the imposition of a particular culture upon individuals or of a particular dominant culture upon another, minority culture via processes of cultural imperialism" Boukli and Copson, 2020: 32). This idea of cultural harm, they note, is readily found in discussions about minority rights and, recently and extensively, in discussions about the criminalisation (or not) of rape pornography.

Finally, cultural harm as misrecognition to:

> the harms that arise from having one's identity challenged, misrepresented or undermined. It is typically derived from a Hegelian idea that, as Nancy Fraser (2000: 109) puts it: "identity is constructed dialogically, through a process of mutual recognition". This is the idea that our subjective sense of our identity and our sense of self is necessarily developed in relation to others.
>
> *(Boukli and Copson, 2020: 33)*

We discuss this as a separate dimension or type of harm, below.

Importantly for Boukli and Copson – and for us – they emphasise that these categories are not discrete but complexly overlapping. For example:

> the harms that are done *to* a culture are often inflicted *by* the imposition of another culture, typically (but not exclusively) by a majority culture on a minority one. Here harm is seen as being done *to* existing culture *by* the claims of another social group. But the harms done *to* and *by* culture also relate to misrecognition, insofar as the infliction of harm *by* and *to* culture is often manifested in the experience of *misrecognition* and the status subordination this entails. These harms of recognition are the symptoms or lived effects of cultural harm.
>
> *(Boukli and Copson, 2020: 33)*

Given this complexity, however, we have decided in this discussion to treat harms of recognition as a category of harms worthy of separate discussion – though we must again emphasise that these 'types' of harm are heuristic devices, isolated for analytical purposes, rather than categories which map on

BOX 3.3 CULTURAL HARM AS HARM TO CULTURE CASE STUDY: THE DAKOTA ACCESS PIPELINE

According to Energy Transfer, the company which oversaw the construction and operation of the pipeline, it is the safest and most efficient means to transport crude oil from the geographically constrained region, providing better access to Gulf Coast and Midwest refineries and other downstream markets, and has been "safely operating since June of 2017", transporting over half a million barrels of oil a day (Data Access Pipeline, n.d.). As well as being a safe and environmentally friendly way of supply oil across a vast region – the pipeline runs for over 1,000 miles – the company claims it is a source of employment and tax revenues (Data Access Pipeline, n.d.).

It may, indeed, be these things. But seen from a different perspective, the construction and operation of the pipeline is a source not only of health, safety, environmental and economic harm, it is a destructive form of cultural harm so that those who occupy the lands across which the pipeline have been constructed – notably the Standing Rock Sioux Tribe Indian reservation – have been engaged in a long political and legal battle, one which received worldwide attention from the summer of 2017 when oil began flowing through the pipeline even though a Federal judge had agreed with the Sioux Tribe that the pipeline's environmental review had been unlawful.

In November 2019, Mike Faith, the chairman of the Standing Rock Sioux Tribe, emphasised the cultural harms entailed in the existence and operation of the pipeline:

> To some, this may be just another pipeline in just another place. But to us, it's not just a pipeline, it's a threat. And it's not just a place, it's our home. The only one we have. Every day the pipeline operates represents a threat to our way of life and an insult to our culture and traditions that have withstood so much. We are still here. We are not giving up this fight.
>
> *(Faith, 2019)*

In fact, the cultural harm was thought to be one which affected Native Americans beyond the Standing Rock Sioux. In 2016, thousands of Native Americans travelled to North Dakota to oppose the construction of the Dakota Access Pipeline through direct action which led to violent confrontations over several years and draconian use of the criminal justice system against many of the protestors.

These protestors had become known as the 'water protectors', and in this term the cultural nature of the struggle in which they were engaged was emphasised. As one of the protestors – an Apache, Lakota, Mexican and African American – said as she camped at Standing Rock through the winter of 2016–2017 to protect the land,

> I feel like I made a commitment to the land and the water, and I found a lot of soul family here ... This is about our safety in this country as people of color and as people indigenous to the land ... If the water gets sick, everyone gets sick.
>
> *(Levin, 2017)*

Herein the particular nature of native American cultures – generally characterised by an intimate relationship to land occupied for thousands of years – is emphasised, and so in turn is the scale of the cultural harm entailed in something like the construction of an enormous oil pipeline across the heart of that land.

simply to the 'real world' – that is clearly not, as Boukli and Copson indicate, the case.

Harms of recognition

As we saw immediately above, Boukli and Copson include recognition harms in their extended definition (typology) of cultural harms. Meanwhile, for Pemberton (2015), some aspects of relational harms relate to the impacts of social processes which misrepresent individuals, specifically those belonging to communities which are demonised or seen as deviant. As Pemberton argues, enforced exclusion from social networks or personal relationships often leads to daily and micro-level impacts – taking part in social activities, inability to secure childcare and ensuring longer-term maintenance of human relationships which may support one's own self-actualisation (2015). In essence, if social structures and surroundings work to limit people's ability to engage with or progress in society, then relational harm is present.

For us, these emphases upon a peculiar form of relational and/or cultural harm highlight the usefulness of including in any typology, as a specific type of harm, *harms of misrecognition*. For Pemberton, such harms arise when public identities are "imposed on people by others within society, and presented as 'spoiled' or 'blemished' in one way or another, so that they are viewed as 'other' and therefore distinct from mainstream society" (Pemberton, 2015: 31), the outcome being that people's ability to engage in said society is reduced, distorted or relationally negatively affected.

These harms of *misrecognition* were defined by Nancy Fraser thus:

> To be denied recognition – or to be 'misrecognised' – is to suffer both a distortion of one's relation to one's self and an injury to one's identity … [It is] … to be denied the status of a full partner in social interaction, as a consequence of institutionalized patterns of cultural value that constitute one as comparatively unworthy of respect or esteem.
>
> *(Fraser, 2000: 109–112)*

In short, misrecognition is "institutionalised subordination" (Fraser, 2000: 114), institutionalised and systematic contempt (Tombs, 2019, 2020) or what Tyler has called social abjection, which results from "violent exclusionary forces of sovereign power; those forces that strip people of their human dignity and reproduce them as dehumanised waste, the disposable dregs and refuse of social life" (Tyler, 2015: 140). We shall return to an extended consideration of such harms later in this chapter, when we consider ontological bases for social harm (but see, for example, Box 3.4).

Autonomy harms

As we shall see below, there is something about harm which relates intimately to blocked capacities, opportunities, the potential for self-realisation or actualisation, and much of this is captured by what Pemberton first termed autonomy harms.

As Canning notes, autonomy is "a facet central to liberty, the freedom to make plans or decisions for oneself without sanction" (2019: 43). For Pemberton, there are many harmful ways in which a person's capacity for autonomous action is undermined and self-actualisation is frustrated or stalled (2015: 29). The first of these is a capacity for understanding and learning, so that people can develop the relevant and appropriate cognitive skills to communicate, critically evaluate and practise their skills. In doing so, one is more likely to lead the life of one's own choosing.

Leading on from this, self-actualisation – the ability of capacity to flourish – is determined by opportunities people have to engage in meaningful and productive social activities (Pemberton, 2015). Self-esteem and

BOX 3.4 HARMS OF RECOGNITION CASE STUDY: THE RISE OF ISLAMOPHOBIA

In the aftermath of the 9/11 attacks on the World Trade Center in New York, representations of Muslims as violent religious fanatics proliferated. By constantly representing Muslims as a 'threat' – both to safety and to democracy – fractures increasingly developed which has exacerbated the social othering of Muslims living in Northern and Oceanian countries, as well as for those migrating who were increasingly seen as an 'invasion' rather than as survivors of conflict or hopeful economic migrants. The conflation between 'Muslim' and 'terrorist' became increasingly embedded in media and political discourse, particularly in the aftermath of numerous attacks by violent fundamentalists in France in 2015 and the UK in 2007 and 2017. Unlike White terror attacks, such as the bombing and shooting attacks perpetrated by White Nationalist Anders Breivik in Norway in 2011, violent attacks by Muslims are more likely to be represented as terrorist attacks. Moreover, it is often this minority of some *violent* people who are taken as representative of Muslims as a whole.

The relational harms developing from this misrecognition have been profound. It has affected relations between Muslim immigrants and communities broadly, as well as settled non-Muslim populations who have increasingly been targeted in attacks since the attacks in Paris in 2015. A recent report by *Tell Mama*, an organisation which measures anti-Muslim attacks, showed more than a 300% increase in attacks in the following week in Britain. These were significantly gendered: as *The Independent* synopsised, "Most victims of the UK hate crimes were Muslim girls and women aged from 14 to 45 in traditional Islamic dress. The perpetrators were mainly white males aged from 15 to 35" (Wright, 2015).

At micro levels, research highlights that some Muslim women no longer feel safe enough to leave their houses at certain times (Canning, 2017), inflicting both relational and autonomy harms. Moreover, the longer-term implications of relational breakdown through – in this case at least – misrepresentation and thus misrecognition can have lethal consequences, as was seen in the mass murder of 50 Muslims who were worshipping in Christchurch, New Zealand, in 2019 and ongoing genocides in China and Myanmar, albeit under different political contexts.

self-worth are often dependent on these opportunities, and thus the reduction or dismantlement of social opportunity negatively affects autonomy. Harms therefore result from role-deprivation and a lack of recognition or reward. Importantly, control over one's own circumstances and value are integral to human development or emotional wellbeing.

Thus, autonomy harms, for Pemberton, are associated with relative and absolute poverty, lack of access to education, employment or training, or precarious working. It is clear in the context of this chapter that autonomy harms are intimately linked to and might be subsumed by other categories. The indicators that Pemberton (2015) chooses to measure the presence or absence of autonomy harms – relative poverty, child poverty, exposure to long working hours and the absence of access to education, employment or training for young people – might all be considered under one or some other categories or types of harm set out here. But it seems to us that, as illustrated in the case of learning care (Box 3.5), there are reasons why this category of harm should be retained and, as Canning's arguments highlight, expanded.

A complex of social harm: border controls in Europe and the United Kingdom

In what follows we present a case study which brings together many of the insights that a social harm approach can add to the examination of a social phenomenon, in this case border controls. The case also illustrates how such an approach has the potential to highlight the interplay of harm at various levels, from the micro through to the meso (institutional) and the macro (structural).

As this chapter has demonstrated, there are many types of harm which can relate to various state and social practices that can have short or long-term consequences. These consequences or outcomes may be interpersonal, such as inflicting emotional harms, but have wider social consequences, such as on families, communities or the workplace. This zemiological framework allows us not only to identify such issues, but to expand our social understanding of how harms may intertwine across intersectional groups and/or at different times in a person or people's lives. As following chapters will note, the aim in doing so should not only be to uncover harms, but to develop modes of responsibility and accountability, and thus the means to mitigate or – ideally – end socially constructed and structural harms.

Considering migration as a trajectory case study, zemiology can help to put the bordering of certain forms of migration into perspective. The concept of 'harm' encompasses many of the issues that affect people's mental,

BOX 3.5 AUTONOMY HARMS: LEARNING CARE

A key feature of autonomy harm is the lack of opportunities for understanding and learning (Pemberton, 2015). Feeley (2014) developed the concept of 'learning care' during a three-year ethnography with survivors of institutional abuses in Irish industrial schools. The study focused on gathering memories of learning literacy in childhoods that were at the extreme end of the affective continuum that extends between care and abuse. What differentiated those in state care who became literate and those who did not was directly linked to degrees of care. Those with some residual family connection often experienced less severe abuse than those who had no one to defend their interests. Learning care was a defining element in becoming literate. Even small amounts of care meant that children were more likely to become literate than were their care-less peers.

A model identified four sources of learning care each of which plays a positive role in learning. Primary learning care is located in the family or alternative care home. Secondary learning care describes the relationships in school and learning centres and solidary or tertiary learning care is experienced, often informally, between peers. Each of these types of learning care is determined, to a large extent, by an underwriting duty of state learning care.

Literacy distribution in the past, and today, mirrors class, gender, ethnic and other hierarchies of wealth, status and power that are the result of state policy (Commission of the European Communities, 2008; OECD, 2009; UNESCO, 2012). Individuals, social groups, communities, schools and entire countries are labelled disadvantaged as if this were a matter of chance rather than the result of political choices. Across the globe, literacy remains the preserve of those who have greatest social privilege. The failure in a state's duty of learning care amounts to an immediate and often lifelong harm and a denial of the autonomous rights of those who experience this learning care inequality.

physical and emotional health. As Hillyard and Tombs (2004: 19) indicate, this is particularly important because:

> Responses to social harms require debates about policy, resources, priorities, and so on. Surely these are more appropriate than relatively

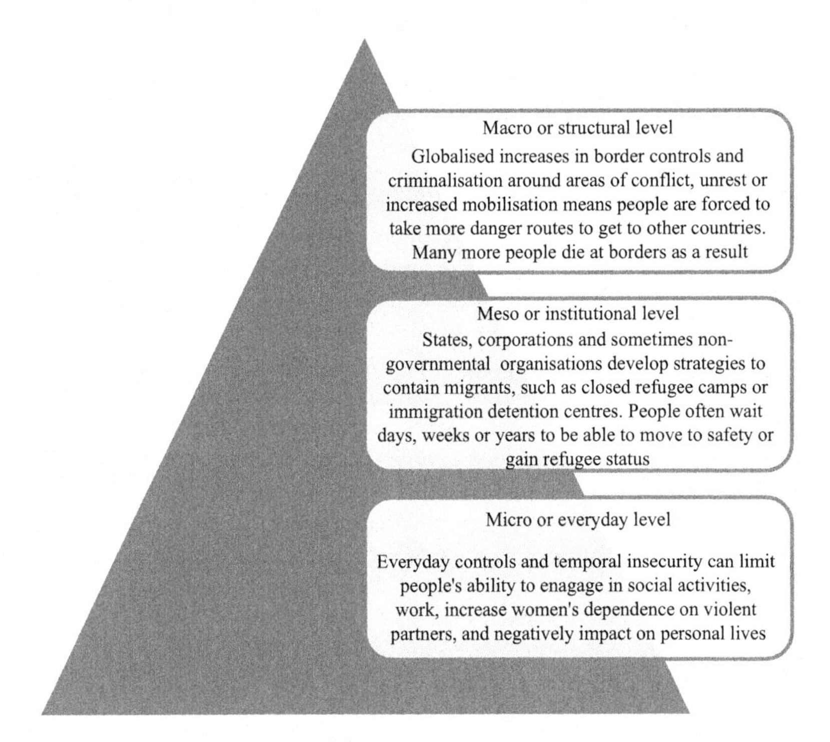

FIGURE 3.2 Forms of controls in the lives of refugee groups

> closed criminal justice systems inhabited by unelected, unaccountable and certainly non-representative elites.

As such, if we begin to move away from a focus on crime and criminology, we are no longer married to the idea that migration and crime are inherently related. We can begin to see the impacts of *illegalisation* of movement – that some people are not able to move freely, even if their lives depend on it, while others (particularly richer people with powerful visas) are able to travel freely for business or leisure.

This brings us then to clearly identifying the harms people experience through and because of border controls. Figure 3.2 does this by considering three levels of controls which people face, from which we will consider the potential for harms in each level.

From a zemiological perspective, we can identify the following examples of harm, using elements of a 'typology' which will be further developed in the following chapter:

Physical harms: the inability to cross borders safely and legally increases the likelihood of people taking riskier journeys, including by sea. Between 2014 and April 2019, at least 31,621 people died at global borders (International Organisation for Migration, 2019). More than half of these were in the Mediterranean. These deaths – and the subsequent emotional harms they cause – can be avoided by making safe and legal routes of passage, as well as investing in conflict resolution and economic support in the countries people flee from, such as Syria, Iraq and Afghanistan. Instead, the European Union ended the use of rescue ships in the Mediterranean, meaning increased likelihood of deaths at sea, and less likelihood of knowing if and when people die as fewer people are there to monitor or acknowledge this.

Economic or financial harms: Increases in border controls can make people more vulnerable to dependence on smugglers, often costing significant amounts of money and generally more than legal travel would. This then facilitates the increase in exploitative networks that use unsafe travel for economic gain. This is often at a huge financial cost to migrants. For those who cannot afford to pay smugglers, even riskier decisions can be made which risk other forms of physical harm – such as selling organs – or emotional harm – such as so-called transactional sex.

Autonomy harms: people living in camps or in immigration detention have little or no autonomy over what they can eat or where they can go and when. For people awaiting the outcome of asylum claims, everyday forms of border controls impact on the ability to take control of their own decisions, affecting how they engage in everyday life.

Temporal harms: people who are 'stuck' at or within borders often feel that their lives and time are being wasted. For many, there is uncertainty for the future. For people who have families who are left in other countries or in conflict areas, the sense of insecurity is constant. People who are living in refugee camps, asylum centres or immigration detention centres often refer to feeling like they are in a state of imprisonment but – instead of counting down on days like a prison sentence – they are counting up, as they do not know when they will have their lives back.

Using border harms as a case study, the extent, dimensions and levels of harmful and potentially treatment becomes clearer. Importantly, this often relates to both institutional and structural violence – in avoidable forms – and results in the mass social harm of deaths in the Mediterranean. Such deaths are captured by Engel's term 'social murder', which he defines thus:

> when society places hundreds of proletarians in such a position that they inevitably meet a too early and an unnatural death, one which is quite as much a death by violence as that by the sword or bullet;

> when it deprives thousands of the necessaries of life, places them under conditions in which they cannot live – forces them, through the strong arm of the law, to remain in such conditions until that death ensues which is the inevitable consequence – knows that these thousands of victims must perish, and yet permits these conditions to remain.
>
> *(Engels, 1845/1969: 86)*

However, most of these harms sit outside of spheres of criminal (or indeed social) justice. As such, we can begin to see the complex and multiple realities – and significance – of a continuum of harm in the context of contemporary borders.

Conclusion

In this chapter we have sought to set out the various categories through which social harm might be identified, understood and considered. We have emphasised, however, that these categories do not exist nor operate discretely. And we have sought to demonstrate that understanding social harm in its various dimensions allows us to develop rich empirical, multi-dimensional representations of harm – quite distinct, for example, to the two-dimensional, inter-personal snapshots which pass for 'crimes'. It perhaps goes without saying, but such complex understandings in turn generate the need for policy responses which are multifaceted, and far from solely dependent upon criminal 'justice'.

Whist setting out as full a typology as possible, we have sought throughout to emphasise that this typology is provisional – to be contested and further developed. In particular, we reiterated the fact that as a provisional schema it is to be refined through the reflections of individuals, households and communities upon the harms they experience and indeed prioritise. This was the praxis originally claimed by Hillyard and Tombs for a social harm approach. This fluidity of 'harm' is a point to which we shall return in the following chapter, since it has implications for any discussion of the ontology of harm. There, we consider how harms are relational before returning to the question, what makes harm harmful?

Note

1 The first workshop addressing this was held in September 2019 in Barcelona. Convened and organised by the Centre for Global Criminology and directed by Henrik Vigh from Copenhagen University, it combined anthropologies with suffering and zemiology and addressed the international drug trade, harms of neoliberalism, border harms and Catalonian resistance movements.

References

Alvesalo, A. (1999) *Meeting the Expectations of the Local Community on Safety – What About White-Collar Crime?*, Paper presented at the 27th Annual Conference of the European Group for the Study of Deviance and Social Control, Palanga, 2–5 September.

Amnesty International (2004) *Clouds of Injustice: Bhopal Disaster Twenty Years On*, Oxford: Amnesty International.

Arcel, L.T. (2003) Introduction, in *Treatment of Torture and Trauma Survivors in a Post-War Society*, edited by L.T. Arcel, S. Popovic, A. Kucukalic and A. Bravo-Mehmedbasic, Sarajevo: Association for Rehabilitation of Torture Victims, 1–11.

Boukli, A. and Copson, L. (2020) Towards a typology of cultural harm: The UK Gender Recognition Act 2004, 'trans fraud', and 'gender deception', *Justice, Power and Resistance*, 3 (2), 26–48.

Boyle, J., ed. (2017) *Psychological Therapies for Survivors of Torture: A Human Rights Approach with People Seeking Asylum*, Monmouth: PCCS Books.

Cain, M. and Howe, A. (2008) *Women, Crime and Social Harm: Towards a Criminology for the Global Era*, Portland: Hart Publishing.

Canning, V. (2016) Unsilencing sexual torture: Responses to refugees and asylum seekers in Denmark, *British Journal of Criminology*, 56 (3), 438–456.

Canning, V. (2017) *Gendered Harm and Structural Violence in the British Asylum System*, Oxon: Routledge.

Canning, V. (2019) *Reimagining Refugee Rights: Addressing Asylum Harms in Britain, Denmark and Sweden*, Migration and Mobilities Bristol, www.statewatch.org/news/2019/mar/uk-dk-se-reimagining-refugee-rights-asylum-harms-3–19.pdf (Accessed 19 June 2020).

Castleman, B. (1979) The export of hazard to developing countries, *International Journal of Health Services*, 9 (4), 569–606.

Chilcot, J. (2016) *The Report of the Iraq Inquiry: Executive Summary*, https://assets.publishing.service.gov.uk/government/uploads/system/uploads/attachment_data/file/535407/The_Report_of_the_Iraq_Inquiry_-_Executive_Summary.pdf (Accessed 19 June 2020).

Commission of the European Communities (CEC) (2008) *Progress Towards the Lisbon Objectives in Education and Training: Indicators and Benchmarks*, Brussels: DGEAC.

Cooper, V. and Whyte, D., eds. (2017a) *The Violence of Austerity*, London: Pluto Press.

Cooper, V. and Whyte, D. (2017b) Introduction, in *The Violence of Austerity*, edited by V. Cooper and D. Whyte, London: Pluto Press, 1–35.

Copson, L. (2018) Beyond 'criminology vs zemiology': Reconciling crime with social harm, in *Zemiology: Reconnecting Crime and Social Harm*, edited by A. Boukli and J. Kotzé, Basingstoke: Palgrave Macmillan, 33–57.

Data Access Pipeline (n.d.) *Moving America's Energy*, https://daplpipelinefacts.com/ (Accessed 14 August 2020).

Dehghan, R. (2018) The health impact of (sexual) torture amongst Afghan, Iranian and Kurdish refugees: A literature review, *Torture Journal*, 28 (3), 77–91.

Dorling, D. (2019) *Inequality and the 1%*, London: Verso.

Engels, F. (1845/1969) *The Condition of the Working Class in England*, Moscow: Panther.

ESRC (2013) *Research Ethics Guidebook*, www.basw.co.uk/resources/research-ethics-guidebook-resource-social-scientists (Accessed 22 September 2020).

Faith, M. (2019) Our fight against the Dakota Access pipeline is far from over, *The Guardian*, 15 November, www.theguardian.com/commentisfree/2019/nov/15/dakota-access-pipeline-standing-rock (Accessed 14 August 2020).

Feeley, M. (2014) *Learning Care Lessons: Literacy, Love, Care and Solidarity*, London: The Tufnell Press.

Fraser, N. (2000) Rethinking recognition, *New Left Review*, 3, 107–120.

Galtung, J. (1969) Violence, peace, and peace research, *Journal of Peace Research*, 6 (3), 167–191.

Garside, R. (2013) Addressing social harm: Better regulation versus social transformation, *Revista Crítica Penal y Poder*, 5, 247–265.

Global Policy Forum (2011) *Economic Consequences*, www.globalpolicy.org/humanitarian-issues-in-iraq/consequences-of-the-war-and-occupation-of-iraq/35722.html#a2011 (Accessed 19 June 2020).

Green, P. and Ward, T. (2004) *State Crime: Governments, Violence and Corruption*, London: Pluto Press.

Herman, J. L. (1992) *Trauma and Recovery: From Domestic Abuse to Political Terror*, London: Pandora.

Hillyard, P. and Tombs, S. (2004) Beyond criminology?, in *Beyond Criminology: Taking Harm Seriously*, edited by P. Hillyard, C. Pantazis, S. Tombs and D. Gordon, London: Pluto Press, 10–29.

International Organisation for Migration (2019) *Missing Migrants Project*, https://missingmigrants.iom.int/ (Accessed 13 October 2020).

Ives, J., ed. (1985) *The Export of Hazard: Transnational Corporations and Environmental Control Issues*, Boston: Routledge and Kegan Paul.

Jones, H. and Cook, K. (2008) *Rape Crisis: Responding to Sexual Violence*, Dorset: Russell House Publishing.

Lasslett, K. (2010) Crime or social harm? A dialectical perspective, *Crime, Law and Social Change*, 54, 1–19.

Laye-Gindhu, A. and Schonert-Reichl, K. A. (2005) Nonsuicidal self-harm among community adolescents: Understanding the 'whats' and 'whys' of self-harm, *Journal of Youth and Adolescence*, 34 (5), 447–457.

Levin, S. (2017) Last stand: 'Water protectors' return to Standing Rock as drilling set to begin, *The Guardian*, 8 February, www.theguardian.com/us-news/2017/feb/08/standing-rock-dakota-access-pipeline-last-stand (Accessed 14 August 2020).

Lloyd, A. (2018) *The Harms of Work*, Bristol: Policy Press.

McDonald, A. (2020) Black parents know 'the talk' too well. It's white parents' turn, *Slate Magazine*, 15 June, https://slate.com/human-interest/2020/06/white-parents-the-talk-racism-police-brutality.html (Accessed 14 August 2020).

Muttitt, G. and Whyte, D. (2016) Tony Blair could face prosecution yet – focus on oil and follow the money, *The Guardian*, 11 July, www.theguardian.com/commentisfree/2016/jul/11/tony-blair-prosecution-war-crimes-hague-geneva-pillage-economy-iraq-chilcot (Accessed 19 June 2020).

OECD (2009) *OECD Programme for International Student Assessment* (PISA). Paris: OECD.

Pearce, F. and Tombs, S. (2012) *Bhopal: Flowers at the Altar of Profit and Power*, Somercoates: Crime Talk Books.

Pemberton, S. (2015) *Harmful Societies: Understanding Social Harm*, Bristol: Policy Press.

Presser, L. (2013) *Why We Harm*, New Brunswick, NJ: Rutgers University Press.

Rejali, D. (2007) *Torture and Democracy*, Princeton, NJ: Princeton University Press.

Ritchie, H. and Roser, M. (2019) Smoking, *Our World in Data*, https://ourworldindata.org/smoking#how-have-smoking-deaths-changed-over-time (Accessed 14 August 2020).

Roberts, D. (2009) *Social Harm and Crime at a Global Level*, London: Centre for Crime and Justice Studies.

Ruggiero, V. (2016) Corporate war crimes, in *The Palgrave Handbook of Criminology and War*, edited by R. McGarry and S. Walklate, London: Palgrave/Macmillan), 61–78.

Short, D. and Szolucha, A. (2017) Fracking Lancashire: The planning process, social harm and collective trauma, *Geoforum*, 98 (1), 264–276.

The Bhopal Medical Appeal (n.d.) *What Happened?* www.bhopal.org/what-happened/ (Accessed 23 January 2011).

Tombs, S. (2018) For pragmatism and politics: Crime, social harm and zemiology, in *Just Harm? Rethinking Zemiology and the Broader Context of Social Harm*, edited by A. Boukli and J. Kotzé, London: Palgrave Macmillan, 11–31.

Tombs, S. (2019) Grenfell: The unfolding dimensions of social harm, *Justice, Power and Resistance*, 3 (1), 61–88.

Tombs, S. (2020) Home as a site of state-corporate violence: Grenfell Tower, aetiologies and aftermaths, *Howard Journal of Crime and Justice*, 59(2), 120–142.

Tyler, I. (2015) *Revolting Subjects: Social Abjection and Resistance in Neo-liberal Britain*, London: Zed Books.

UNESCO (2012) *Adult and Youth Literacy: UIS Report 20*, Paris: UNESCO.

Watson Institute of International and Public Affairs and Brown University (2018) *Costs of War: Iraqi Citizens*, https://watson.brown.edu/costsofwar/costs/human/civilians/iraqi (Accessed 19 June 2020).

Whyte, D. (2007) The crimes of neo-liberal rule in occupied Iraq, *The British Journal of Criminology*, 47 (2), 177–195.

World Health Organisation (2020) *Tobacco*, 27 May, www.who.int/news-room/fact-sheets/detail/tobacco (Accessed 14 August 2020).

Wright, O. (2015) Paris attacks: Women targeted as hate crime against British Muslims soars following terrorist atrocity, *The Independent*, 22 November, www.independent.co.uk/news/uk/home-news/paris-attacks-british-muslims-face-300-spike-in-racial-attacks-in-week-following-terror-a6744376.html (Accessed 19 June 2020).

Yar, M. (2012) Critical criminology, critical theory and social harm, in *New Directions in Criminological Theory*, edited by S. Hall and S. Winlow, London: Routledge, 52–65.

Zedner, L. (2011) Putting crime back on the criminological agenda, in *What Is Criminology?*, edited by C. Hoyle and M. Bosworth, Oxford: Oxford University Press, 271–283.

4

THE RELATIONS AND ONTOLOGIES OF HARM

Introduction

Having, in the previous chapter, set out an extended typology of different 'categories' of harms, in this chapter we wish to consider some of the characteristics or features of harms. At the same time, this focus on the characteristics of harms is also a way of further exploring how harm 'works' and indeed how harms are experienced.

In the first part of the chapter, we argue that harms are relational – they have spatial and temporal dimensions. They also operate synergistically – that is, different forms of harm can co-exist and create heightened or new forms of harms. Further, they operate according to hierarchy, through hierarchical relations, here exemplified via their racialised and gendered effects, as well as the ways in which harms reflect the separations between humans and both their natural environment and from other non-human animals.

From there we review efforts to determine the ontology of harm. That review traverses in particular contributions made by Pemberton (2015), Raymen (2019), Soliman (2019) and Yar (2012), as a result of which we conclude that while there is clearly no agreed ontology of harm – there remains a great deal of conceptual work to be done here – there are nonetheless some key, emergent points of agreement on what the contours of such an ontology look like.

Harms as relational

Time, space and place

The emphasis that harms tend to have a relational quality is perhaps captured by the observation that harms, like benefits or advantages, have a distributive element to them. That is, where harm occurs or exists, and there is an individual or group who are harmed, this harm is usually related to a benefit – direct or otherwise – to another individual or group. This therefore sees harm as a social relation. Relations of benefits and harms are generally more accessible – more immediate – where the relationships between the parties to the harm are proximate in time and space – and this is generally the case in many of the harms that classify as 'crimes', as we discussed in Chapter 2.

But in the case of many of the kinds of harms which we have discussed in this book, there are frequently enormous distances between the source and object of the harm, the 'offender' and 'victim', in terms of both space and time – yet this is not to deny the relationship between these, merely that it is not so immediately apparent. As we have indicated previously, these dimensions of distance rather than proximity run entirely contrary to our stories of crime, to the ways in which criminal law is constructed and, indeed, more generally, to how we think of causal relations.

If these sound esoteric observations, it should, for example, be clear that it is impossible to make sense of the harms experienced by African Americans in contemporary USA without relating these to the historical fact and legacies of colonialism and slavery. Or, in a contemporary sense, we cannot understand the experiences of Indigenous farmers, land-owners and workers in the export-crop-producing states of, for example, South America or West Africa without a recognition of the way in which the global food industry is structured, the predominance of Western Transnational Corporations and relations of coloniality between the Global North and Global South (Tombs, 2020). More generally, we would argue that understanding the distributions of harms requires an understanding of north-south relations and relations of coloniality – even if we focus on the local, such as why the majority of those who died in Grenfell Tower were people of colour, and almost a half of the residents of the tower had come to the UK from another country of birth. Harms have a spatial and a geographical dimension.

To say that harms have both a spatial and a temporal quality is to claim not just that that they operate thus but that they are experienced in these ways too. That is, their effects, intensity, nature shift over time and through geographical location – the experience of harm can diminish or increase or both over time or through different locations. Moreover, the form which harm takes can and does change over time. So, for example, a physical harm can generate detrimental emotional or psychological, as well as financial, effects and in some instances, where the result of an injury or illness is severe and results in permanent 'disability', harms of misrecognition can be generated.

The temporal and spatial qualities of harms also alert us to the fact that harms operate and are experienced synergistically – harms extend through time and space and in so doing they encounter each other and are experienced synergistically, in more searing forms, such as, for example, where physical harms are experienced along with long-term, increasingly detrimental emotional and psychological harms which can affect those around the harmed or indeed those in other geographical locales who may see themselves as vulnerable to similar forms of harm.

In a sense, all of these observations are an obviousness – harm is not necessarily a time-bound event but a process, so that physical, emotional, cultural and so on effects are felt and persist over time. But it is important to state this obviousness given the social prevalence of attempts to curtail this temporal quality of harms – so dominant social processes provide justice for some harms (crimes), recompense through insurance companies for others (financial loss), emotional support services provide closure for yet others (bereavement). But these temptations of curtailment rather belie how harms can not just affect but indeed recreate our being and biographies in ways that are irrevocable.

Harms can also be experienced as temporal in other, quite direct ways – where the manipulation of, or lack of control over, time is a source of harm itself (Bhatia and Canning, 2021). Temporality is experienced differently by people at different stages of their life. Temporality relates to time, a sense of security or control, and the ability to use time to one's own means and advantage. Many social aspects can impact on how people spend their time, and whether time is experienced positively. Uncertainty for the immediate or long-term future can reduce people's capacity to engage in meaningful activities, or to make plans for the kind of future that they want for themselves and/or their families.

BLM we take everyday examples of waiting without knowing when an outcome is due, it is easy to see that uncertainty can cause stress (see, for example, Box 4.1). In universities, students often cite waiting for the outcome of an assessment as a period of stress or anxiety. Familial stress often relates to time – of waiting for a paycheque or welfare allowance and not knowing if it will be available in time for bill payments. These are not indicators or outcomes of harm, but rather an illustrative example of how we – as individuals – can be affected by temporal uncertainty. In a stark and novel discussion

BOX 4.1 TEMPORAL HARM CASE STUDY: REDUCTIONS IN FAMILY REUNIFICATION RIGHTS FOR REFUGEES IN SWEDEN

Reaching safety is a key priority for people seeking asylum. During the increase in refugee arrivals in Europe in 2015 and 2016, many people made their way north to Sweden, where a social democratic government was initially keen to support the wellbeing of people seeking asylum. As the arrivals into the country began to peak, reaching 162,000 people, the Swedish government changed numerous policies and laws to reduce the number of people entering or staying.

One such law was the right to family reunification. Where many people had arrived with the intention of applying to have their families moved safely under reunification policies, the right to reunification was made almost impossible, including relatively high incomes and affording only some forms of refugee status the right to apply. The obvious – and intended - outcome of this was that many families were no longer able to travel to Sweden to reunite. However, a secondary outcome was that people who had made it to safety no longer felt a sense of certainty, since they could not guarantee the safety of their families. Rather than using this time to adjust to a new life, many people went on to experience temporal harm as they worried about the potential loss of family at borders or left in conflict zones. The potential for anxiety, stress, mental illness and symptoms related to Post-Traumatic Stress Disorder were therefore made worse, having longer-term temporal harms on people and affected the time that families would spend together, and indeed ensure safety of those left behind.

of temporal harms, Iliadou, in *The Lived Experiences of Border Crossers in Lesvos Island*, explores the violent harms of 'stuckedness and waiting'. She argues that these are deliberate techniques enforced by EU policy makers upon border crossers in Lesbos to "(i) regulate, discipline, govern and control the undesirable border crossers; (ii) to mentally exhaust them by making their lives unliveable in order to deter them from coming, staying or moving further to Europe" (Iliadou, 2019: 16).

Temporal harm therefore relates not only to a loss of this control or of social opportunities, but can actually compound – or make worse – people's physical or mental and emotional health. As Canning (2017) highlights, this is particularly the case for people who have experienced traumatic histories or inter-personal violence such as sexual abuse, sustained or repeat violences or torture.

Racialised harms

A further specific dimension of relational harms that we wish to consider here are racialised harms. The Black Lives Matter movement erupted into global prominence in May 2020 when an African American, George Floyd, was killed during an arrest in Minneapolis by a police officer who forced his knee down into Floyd's neck for almost 9 minutes, causing death by asphyxiation.

BLM states that its "mission is to build local power and to intervene in violence inflicted on Black communities by the state and vigilante" (Black Lives Matter, n.d.). It is interesting in the light of the critique of crime and criminal justice on which this text is founded that BLM makes its key element of the struggle for racial justice a targeting of police violence. In the wake of the killing of George Floyd, a key demand became the defunding of the police:

> We call for an end to the systemic racism that allows this culture of corruption to go unchecked and our lives to be taken.
>
> We call for a national defunding of police. We demand investment in our communities and the resources to ensure Black people not only survive, but thrive. If you're with us, add your name to the petition right now and help us spread the word.
>
> *(Black Lives Matter, 2020b)*

BLM is generally considered to have its immediate origins in the killing of Trayvon Martin, a 17-year-old killed by a local neighbourhood watch volunteer in Florida in 2012. Black Lives Matter seeks to confront the institutionalised and structural racism of the USA – a society built on slavery. It is a society where Black people are imprisoned at nearly six times the rate of white people, and African Americans are more than twice as likely to be killed by police when unarmed than white Americans (Ramaswamy, 2017). Such racial disparities and racialised harms are hardly confined to the USA of course, but are global and long-standing – that is, with clear spatial and temporal dimensions.

Just weeks before the killing of George Floyd, BLM had been prominent in the USA in exposing the racial disparities in deadly exposure to Covid-19 (Black Lives Matter, 2020a). Almost simultaneously, the UK Government's Office for National Statistics was revealing that Black Britons were "more than four times more likely to die from the disease than white people, with Pakistanis and Bangladeshis almost twice as likely to die compared to the white majority" (Booth and Barr, 2020).

Crucially, racialised harms are relational – racial injustice and the harms which are experienced by people of colour are only explicable in the context of white privilege. Following Leonardo (2009), Bhopal defines white privilege as "the expression of whiteness through the maintenance of power, resources, accolades and systems of support through formal and informal structures and procedures" and:

> is maintained, and often obscured, through white peoples' rationalisations in using broad (often racist) categorisations of people of colour and lack of cultural sensitivity. White privilege maintains itself through people's actions and existing structural procedures, which propagate unequal outcomes for people of colour.
>
> *(Bhopal, 2018: 19)*

Thus:

> white privilege is instrumental to racism … Racism's legacy does not exist without purpose. It brings with it not just a disempowerment for those affected by it but an empowerment for those who are not. That is white privilege. Racism bolsters white peoples' life chances. It affords an unearned power; it is designed to maintain a quiet dominance.
>
> *(Eddo-Lodge, 2018: 115–116)*

Racialised harm can therefore be understood as relational.

Gendered harms

One further, specific dimension of relational harms is gendered harms – those harms which relate to processes, structures or experiences as a result of gendered inequalities and which have gendered impacts. As feminists have long evidenced, inequalities in society are both experienced and enacted across gendered lines. This is the same for gendered harm. For example, this can mean disproportionate experiences of domestic or sexual violence, in that women are statistically subject to abuse and lethal violence, whilst men are disproportionately the perpetrators of this violence. This is not to say that no men are subjected to such violence, or that no women perpetrate it, but rather that certain structural fabrics facilitate and exacerbate such violence in ways that gendered patterns can be seen.

At this point, one might ask why the term crime would not be used in the context of such violence, and indeed for some scenarios it would. However, as Cain and Howe demonstrated, harm often goes unseen or unregulated even after a formal 'crime' has taken place (2008). Likewise, certain forms of violence remain legal in many countries, including rape in marriage and domestic violence. Even in countries where violence against women and/or LGBTQI people is heavily regulated or criminalised, the prevalence and disproportionality of gendered abuse remains palpable. This includes for example countries such as the United Kingdom where the numbers of women murdered by men has not reduced from the 1970s, even though there has been a significant expansion in the use of law to criminalise male violence against women. As such, significant social change might be better placed to happen beyond the realms of states and legislation if gendered harms are to be eradicated.

A gendered harm approach thus requires us to look at social phenomena from gendered perspectives (Canning, 2017). Alongside the seemingly obvious forms of harm (indeed, violence) outlined above, a gendered harm lens requires us to think critically of ways in which structural decisions also have gendered implications (Box 4.2). For example, cuts to welfare entitlements may lead to (supposedly) unintended but foreseeable outcomes such as increasing women's financial reliance on violent partners.

Environmental harms

A further specific dimension of relational harms that we wish to consider here are anthropocentric harms, that is those harms – often known as environmental harms – which result from the interaction of human animals with other species and the natural environment. Environmental harms are resultant of social processes which have a negative impact on the environment, humans, non-human species and the ecosystem. This form of harm has become increasingly recognisable in mainstream media and social consciousness: as a species, we are now long past the luxury of overlooking the realities faced by Earth's natural world and resources. Indeed, we are even past the stage of overlooking the impacts of increased environmental harms on those who are most affected: the plant and animal kingdom, Indigenous people and areas of the Global South which disproportionately receive pollution from the Global North whilst simultaneously having regional resources extracted for capitalistic interests, exemplified in Box 4.3.

We have entered a unique age: the age of the Anthropocene. Whilst earlier shifts in localised and global climates were almost exclusively induced by natural causes, the negative changes affecting the planet now stem

BOX 4.2 GENDERED AND RACIALISED HARM CASE STUDY: INDIGENOUS WOMEN'S EXPERIENCES OF GENDERED HARMS IN SOUTH AMERICA

As Andrea Smith argued, the gendered implications of harmful processes or decisions are often overlooked, both in their existence and in their severity. She notes that "the criminal justice system has always been brutally oppressive toward communities of colour" (2015: 155; see also Davis, 2008). As such, understanding or responding to such violences through state-sanctioned criminal justice are not always optimal or appropriate, specifically when it is the state or state actors which enact or sanction violence in the first place.

Looking at historically oppressive conditions to which Indigenous women have been subject, we are able to see not only structural and inter-personal violence, but a litany of long-term harms which have intrinsically gendered consequences. Take, for example, the justification of increased birth control and forced sterilisation of Native American women's bodies as a means to curb increases in welfare expenditure and education and instead control in the USA and later South America (specifically Indigenous women in Peru, and disproportionately Quechua and Aymara).

These decisions were gendered and indeed racialised, and the impacts encompassed emotional, physical and medical harms on non-consenting women. Women lost autonomy over their bodies and futures, endured psychological harms based on social experimentation, and longer-term consequences such as dependence on counteractive drugs and medication. Harms were sexualised in nature, inducing psychological harm through shame of forced undressing for some, and even death through inadequate hygiene conditions for others.

disproportionately from human activity, through pollution, CO_2 emissions (including over-farming of livestock) and the burning of fossil fuels. The outcome is the gradual demise of coral reefs, significant depletions across animal and plant species and the increase in uncontrolled bushfires (in Australia, for example, these have been responsible for the deaths of more than 500 million animals in late 2019/2020 alone). Meanwhile expansive burning of the Amazon Rainforest – not a natural phenomenon – is increasingly done by states and corporations with impunity to enable space for corporate capital

BOX 4.3 ENVIRONMENTAL HARM CASE STUDY: SHELL OIL SPILL IN THE OGONI DELTA, NIGERIA

Since 1958 the British-Dutch company Shell has led oil drilling operations in the Ogoniland region of the Niger Delta, Nigeria. Once an area of natural beauty and with high levels of farming and fish reserves, it has been subject to multiple oil spills. Vanguard reports that:

- There were about 7,000 oil spills between 1970 and 2000.
- The Nigerian Oil Spill Monitor recorded some 5,296 oil spills between January 2005 and July 2014.
- As of 2010, Royal Dutch Shell admitted to having spilled nearly 14,000 tons (about 100,000 barrels of oil) which was mainly across the oil-rich Ogoni, made up of a total of 18 communities in four local government areas.
- Amnesty International estimates total oil spill in the Ogoni to be between 9 and 13 million barrels, with Shell and ENI, the Italian multinational oil giant, admitting to more than 550 oil spills in 2014 alone (see Vanguard, 2018).

The environmental impacts of the spills have been devastating to the region, with sanctions on planting crops in some areas and significant depletions in farm and fishing stocks. Whilst Amnesty International estimates that a clean-up will take approximately 30 years (Amnesty International, 2015) the actual environmental harms are unprecedented in the area, with some species unlikely to ever recover.

From a criminological perspective, significant steps have been taken against the multinational giant Shell, specifically in its complicity in the unlawful arrest, detention and hanging of rights activists known as the Ogoni Nine.

From a zemiological perspective, the harm experienced in this region is inherently environmental, but it is also a case which creates many more *social* harms. Illness and skin diseases have increased in the region (physical harms); food supplies have diminished for many local communities to eat or trade (economic and physical harms); some communities living locally have been forced to move (relational harms). The extent of the environmental harms inflicted over decades in the region caused will likely impact on regional ecosystems for generations to come.

through logging, agricultural farming and soya production. The impact of this increase in fires – up 60 per cent to 93,000 between 2018 and 2019 – has caused untold destruction to animal life, habitat loss and indigenous communities (Evans, 2019). Climate catastrophe is an existential threat – we are in the midst of the era of ecocide (Whyte, 2020).

Like Large (2018) and Tombs and Whyte (2015), many green criminologists highlight that there is an urgency required to regulate states and corporations that are accountable for contributing to and sustaining environmental harms (see Goyes, 2019; Sollund, 2012; South and Brisman, 2013; Walters, 2011, 2018; White, 2018). However, the extent of such harms is now having unprecedented impacts. As both Walters (2018) and White (2018) argue, a social harm perspective gives us the potential for documenting otherwise unseen or invisible harms at micro levels. A specifically zemiological perspective would thus facilitate in-depth investigation into the everyday harms caused by or contributing to a range of emerging social problems, for example, pollution-related respiratory problems, land loss or forced displacement. As with the development of an anthropological zemiology discussed in the introduction of this chapter, there is clear potential for merging zemiological insight with perspectives outside of the criminological, such as human geography, environmental sciences and even zoology. As the following chapter will go on to note, in cases of extreme harms such as endemic environmental harms, zemiology moves from a self-contained discipline to a socially scientific lens through which we can more easily and effectively identify, map, and address and potentially resist harm.

Humanocentric harms

A final specific dimension of relational harms that we wish to consider here are humanocentric harms, that is, harms to non-human animals. Often treated as a sub-set of environmental harms (see, for example, Sollund, 2015; Wyatt, 2013), more recent work has identified an 'animal turn' across the social sciences (Peggs, 2012). Focusing upon this, Cole has recently described humanocentrism as "the belief that humans are more important than other living things, including other animals. From a humanocentric perspective, the importance given to other animals varies according to their perceived usefulness to humans" (Cole, 2020: 115). Thus, for Cole, and others, critical attention is required to the interconnections between humans and other animals – it is in these interconnections, these *relations*, that we perceive inequalities and systematic harm production, such as those quantified in Box 4.4.

BOX 4.4 CASE STUDY EXAMPLE: HARMS OF ANIMAL EXPERIMENTATION

According to Cruelty Free International, "Millions of animals are used and killed in the name of progress every year."

It estimates that at least a staggering 192.1 million animals were used for scientific purposes worldwide in 2015. This figure includes an estimated 79.9 million experiments on animals as well as millions of other animals who are killed for their tissues, used to breed genetically modified animal strains and bred but not used or killed as surplus. According to its analysis, the top 10 animal testing countries in the world are China (20.5 million) Japan (15.0 million), the United States (15.6 million), Canada (3.6 million), Australia (3.2 million), South Korea (3.1 million), the United Kingdom (2.6 million), Brazil (2.2 million), Germany (2.0 million) and France (1.9 million), in that order.

However, it is worth noting that the products which develop from such tests are not necessarily contained in each country and instead, given globalisation and cross-border trade, often end up at our doorsteps.

It calculated the total number of experiments involving dogs and monkeys worldwide. In 2015, an estimated 207,724 tests using dogs and 158,780 tests using monkeys were conducted. The top 10 users of dogs were: China; the United States; Canada; South Korea; Japan; Australia; Brazil; the United Kingdom; Germany and India. The top 10 users of monkeys were: the United States; China; Japan; Brazil; Canada; the United Kingdom; France; Germany; India and South Korea.

Harm is therefore central to testing and experimentation in many of these forms, including the physical harms of medicalisation or poor treatment, as well as the potential for emotional or psychological harms on animals in distress, as well as those administering potentially painful experiments.

(Cruelty Free International, nd)

Cole examines a variety of these harmful relations, noting that large numbers of non-human animals are harmed by the routine operation of many social structures – which he therefore conceptualises as 'social harms':

> A range of social structures legally and directly harm nonhuman animals, from scientific research to sport and entertainment. For example,

> experimentation on live nonhuman animals in the pharmaceutical industry. Worldwide, this is estimated to involve around 115 million nonhuman animals annually … The campaigning organization Animal Aid has maintained a Race Horse Death Watch website since 2007, which has recorded 1,965 deaths of horses on UK race courses as I write … Social harms also afflict other animals as unintended collateral damage. For instance, motorised transport entails the killing and injuring of other animals (as well as human accident victims), often described as 'road kill'.
>
> *(Cole, 2020: 121)*

Cole focuses in particular upon 'livestock' farming and fishing, the legal activities that kill more non-human animals than any other human activity, resulting in hundreds of billions of deaths every year, as well as non-lethal harms that have physical, mental and emotional dimensions. Further, 'livestock' farming and fishing generate environmental harms which include: depletion of land and water resources; water and air pollution, including greenhouse gas emissions; and collateral harms such as 'bycatch', killing of non-target creatures during commercial fishing. In so doing, he identities an animal-industrial complex as a key concept for analysing the interconnecting social structures that construct demand for 'animal products'. This term:

> refers to the harmful exploitation of nonhuman animals on an industrial scale, and how different industries are inter-related within legal, state-sanctioned frameworks, so that together they form a 'complex'. More recently, the animal-industrial complex was defined by sociologist Richard Twine as a, "partly opaque and multiple set of networks and relationships between the corporate (agricultural) sector, governments, and public and private science. With economic, cultural, social and affective dimensions it encompasses an extensive range of practices, technologies, images, identities and markets."
>
> *(Cole, 2020: 128)*

The complex is based around coalitions of transnational corporations whose profitability is dependent on the exploitation of non-human animals; these companies in turn depend on state-maintained infrastructure, subsidies and legal frameworks to ensure their smooth operation; and the animal-industrial complex also depends on the media construction of positive associations between 'animal product' consumption and consumers' identities and relationships – in ways which deny and obscure harms.

The ontological bases of harm?

Finally, in this chapter, having set out a variety of forms, sites and dimensions of harm, and having rejected a rights-based ontology for defining social harm in the previous chapter, we need to return to the question still begged by that rejection – that is, what is to be the basis for identifying a phenomenon as 'harmful' or a 'social harm', and thus falling within the legitimate ambit of zemiology?

There are several observations to make here.

First, as we have already argued in Chapter 2, in an empirical sense we know a great deal about social harm, and can know a great deal more.

Second, as we have indicated in the previous and in this chapter, we can say a great deal, too, about types of social harm, the different fora in which these play out, and the relational characteristics which typically imply who is more rather than less likely to experience these, while, at the same time, having these understandings continually informed by the reflexive experiences of those subject to harms (but see Box 4.5).

Third, however, none of this is to address what makes harm harmful in any definitive ontological sense. So let us briefly consider some of the responses that have been developed to this question.

For Pemberton, in his original discussion of this question, the answer is to be found in a theory of human needs. Using Doyal and Gough's (1991) classic work, Pemberton (2007) and Pantazis and Pemberton (2009) argue that harm is perpetuated when specified needs are not fulfilled. It is not clear, however, how invoking a theory of 'needs' gets potential zemiologists out of the ontological woods. However sympathetic one may be to Doyal and Gough's conceptualisation of needs, it is hardly unproblematic. Indeed, one of the oft-raised objections to any attempt to identify a theory of human need is that once this shifts from the most abstract universal statements to the level of adding greater specificity to identifying such needs, then any such exercise almost inevitably descends into relativism. This was one of the central topics of the celebrated exchange between Kate Soper in response to Doyal and Gough's formulation (Soper, 1993; Doyal, 1993), it was also raised more recently by Lasslett (2010) in response to Pemberton's (and others') centring of a theory of social harm or zemiology around needs.

Subsequently, Pemberton (2015) attempted to operationalise a needs approach to harm (see also Copson, 2011, and above). While in so doing he provides insightful and persuasive analyses of the performance of a number of selected states and regimes in relation to a range of harms, the theoretical work of grounding the latter in the context of needs remains rather overlooked. There is no doubt that he advances our empirical understanding of the distribution of social harm considerably, while the text demonstrates the potential of a paradigm within which social harm is central but which is neither linked to, nor reliant upon, law, jurisprudence or some other legal framework. But at the same time his work underscores the fact that a zemiology is very much in its infancy, a work in progress at best (Tombs, 2015).

In this respect, one aspect of the challenge indicated by Richard Garside, in one of the more careful and critical analyses of the ideas to date, remains to be taken up:

> A critical challenge for social harm scholarship is to apply its insights on the social and relational nature of social harm – the fact that its mediations are concrete and material, not natural nor merely political or ideological – and its connection to human need, through the development of a clear and coherent understanding of the social production and reproduction of harm in the material processes of capital accumulation.
>
> *(Garside, 2013: 257)*

That is, we can continue to develop insights on the nature of harm, a key focus of this book through conceptual discussion but also via the empirical reference points, evidence and case studies embedded throughout. Further, there have been attempts to relate these to the material processes of specific forms of capitalist production – see, for example, Hillyard and Tombs' (2004) attempt to map out a political economy of harm under globalising neo-liberalism, two thoughtful edited collections on harm production under neo-liberalism (Mitchell *et al.*, 2019, Pantazis *et al.*, 2019) or, very differently, Hall and Winlow's (2018) ultra-realist demand to transcend a myopic focus on the 'big trouble' or 'little evils' of neo-liberalism. But what significantly remains to be addressed in Garside's challenge is the ontological connecting of social harm to human need.

This is partly to say that, in our view, we can reflect very fruitfully upon the question of what makes harm harmful and how we recognise harm without setting out an ontology of harm *per se*. This may be a provisional state of affairs – beyond the scope of this text but something to be determined or achieved subsequently. Or, it may be that interrogating the question rather than reaching an answer is the key here: it might be a productive process without endpoint, so that what is experienced as harm, recognised as harm, and approximates some of the criteria discussed in this chapter to date, therefore counts as harm in an empirical sense, perhaps always subject to challenge, contest, confirmation and in the absence of any epistemological or ontological certainties?

That said, in one thoughtful analysis of the potential of zemiology, Yar has argued that "the lack of specificity in our analysis leaves the concept of harm lacking the very same ontological reality that is postulated as grounds for rejecting the concept of crime" (2012: 59). In short, zemiology has thus far failed to define what makes something 'a harm' or harmful and how harmful outcomes differ from non-harmful ones. He suggests that the concept of 'recognition' can deal with this deficit in our theorisation and that it is possible to establish the basic needs that form human integrity and wellbeing. Harm occurs when there is no recognition of these basic needs. Harms, in this sense, reflect disrespect.

Yar draws upon the critical theory of the Frankfurt School and in particular Honneth's critical theory of recognition, within which self-realisation is viewed as an inter-subjective endeavour, dependent upon self-esteem as a result of mutual recognition of each other's autonomy, freedom and human value – all generating a vision of a just society (Yar, 2012: 57).

Yar argues that a theory of recognition can ground a theory of social harm in establishing those human needs which need to be met to ensure a human flourishing in an Aristotelian sense (Yar, 2012: 59) – harm ensues from the denial of this recognition and these needs.

Where Yar becomes problematic is, first, in his stated aim to use this conceptualisation to dissolve the juxtaposition of crime and harm as "competing and non-compatible conceptual alternatives" (Yar, 2012: 60). Then, second, he seeks to do so by rescuing the category of law from that which defines crimes from the viewpoint of power to that which guarantees, can anticipate or encapsulate progressive moral principles through legal rights which themselves prevent "those recognitive needs that Honneth defines a identified with the dignity of the person" (Yar, 2012: 62). In this way, "we can evaluate the common categories of crime as legitimate (or illegitimate) with reference to the basic needs of social subjects" (Yar, 2012: 62). Thus, while acknowledging that the criminal law can be conceived as "a coercive instrument legitimated by the power of the capitalist state", Yar (2012: 61) argues that it is possible to adopt a different view of the law using a recognition theoretical standpoint. From this position, law is an attempt, however "partial, flawed or misguided", to enshrine formal codes and prohibitions to protect people from harm and assist in securing their basic rights. Yar, then, concludes with a clear appeal to the law in defining harm. On this basis he considers zemiology as a promising orientation but within critical criminology, a view we reject.

It is also worth pointing to the observation by Yar on the need to "avoid 'flattening' … diverse experiences of harm into a single kind" (Yar, 2012: 60), thus harm needs to be defined and theorised in a way which:

> retains a crucial sensitivity to the different orders of forms of need that we experience as humans (love, respect, esteem) and we can allocate

> different harms to the appropriate order or kind of recognitive needs that are being violated. Recognition can thus perform the analytical work of describing and classifying social harms and problems according to the specific needs that they refuse. Moreover, it can perform the moral evaluative work of assessing different social arrangements, actions, and institutionalised processes according to the extent to which they succeed or fail in satisfying those needs whose realisation is essential for human flourishing.
>
> *(Yar, 2012: 60)*

So we can agree with Yar, whether or not 'recognition' is the theoretical basis for so doing, that the documenting, classifying of harms is crucial, as is a flexible approach to so doing, one which can recognise the diverse experiences of those who are harmed. Another analysis of the ontological basis of harm, by Francesca Soliman, also acknowledges the benefits of conceptual flexibility. Thus we can agree with Soliman when she states that a "loose understanding of social harm provides an attractive degree of flexibility when contrasted with the problematic power relations hiding within the more rigid definition of crime". But we would not at all share the caveat that she adds to this, somewhat echoing Yar's commitment to zemiology within critical criminology, namely: "however, it also risks promoting a view of zemiology as antithetical, rather than complementary, to criminology" (Soliman, 2019: 10).

As we noted, Yar (2012) had sought an ontological basis for zemiology by building on Honneth's theory of recognition, which proposes recognition at familial, community and state level – echoing the sociological tradition of focusing on the micro, meso and macro (Canning, 2017). As Soliman outlines, this usefully highlights the "interpersonal acts, structural impediments, and wider processes that deny the pre-conditions leading to individual self-realisation at any of the levels conceptualised as harms, as they deny fundamental human need" (2019: 11).

Following from Canning's call for a move towards the development of border zemiology (2018), Soliman seeks to outline "what a zemiological methodology should look like, or upon which ontological and epistemological grounding it should be based" (Soliman, 2019: 10). Following Yar, and in turn his use of Honneth's work, Soliman argues that a theory of recognition can "give coherence to the concept of social harm" (Soliman, 2019: 11) but seeks to transcend this. This is necessary, she argues, because recognition both posits an atomised individual and at the same time an individual who is only constructed socially. She therefore turns to Gidden's theory of structuration to resolve this agency-structure contradiction and agents, according to which agents and structures simultaneously create one another.

Further, to capture a recognition-based understanding of social harm requires a version of Margaret Archer's 'analytical dualism', "where agency and structure are ontologically distinct and co-create each other not simultaneously, but over time" (Soliman, 2019: 13). Methodologically, she continues, such an approach implies resort to the critical realism of Bhaskar and others – but what is of interest for us is her reference to Bhaskar's concept of absence:

> absence is not just the negation of a state, but a state in itself, and as such it can generate consequences. Furthermore, ills can be seen as absences of an ideal state, just like social harm is here conceptualized as absence of recognition, and these absences can limit human realization … Human emancipation therefore requires the removal of these ill-causing absences, and of the constraints that may inhibit this removal … A recognition-based, critical realist zemiology thus revolves around a political view of the social world, and the progressive struggle to remove obstacles to human realization.
>
> *(Soliman, 2019: 14)*

In terms of what this ideal state within which human realisation is possible looks like, Soliman turns to Nancy Fraser's work on misrecognition and her emphasis on its related fundamental dimension of social injustice: 'distributive injustice', or maldistribution. "Misrecognition and maldistribution, while distinct, are closely linked: both need to be included in a vision of justice, as addressing one will not ameliorate the other. The definition of social harm must therefore include both dimensions" (Soliman, 2019: 16).

Fraser had indeed located her theory of recognition within what she called a 'status' model rather than an 'identity' model since the former mitigated the necessary trajectory of the latter, namely to "displace struggles for redistribution" (Fraser, 2000: 119). Misrecognition entails cultural harm, but the latter is not 'free-standing', but linked to distributive injustice. Thus, for her, struggles for recognition must simultaneously be – and are only progressive alongside – struggles for economic justice. The good – least harmful – society is, *inter alia*, one of the greatest economic justice.

A final analysis we discuss makes some similar observations, also raising the significance of flourishing and self-realisation, also engaging with the need to identify a vision of a better, fairer more just society, within which to ground a concept of harms – albeit these are reached by a very different theoretical route. As with other commentators, Raymen (2019) begins by forensically summarising the problem with social harm as a concept and therefore zemiology as discipline based upon it. Thus, while he recognises that "theoretical principles of social harm" have been determined which are "more or less coherent", these principles are incapable of adequately distinguishing between more or less serious forms of social harm – between those which "should be considered genuinely harmful" in contrast to the "mildly injurious". Such determinations require secure ontological and ethical bases which take us beyond the intuitive claim that we know harm when we see it. That is, "social harm as a concept is sustained by its intuitive moral-political appeal and 'common-sense' purchase, but no more" (Raymen, 2019: 135).

However, Raymen's way out of this conceptual, theoretical and ontological impasse is not, as he puts it, "a little more research, democratic debate, and tinkering with regards to our technical application of this concept" so that "a definitional consensus could be seen to be within reach" (Raymen, 2019: 136). The failure to reach a consensus is, for Raymen, following Žižek and Badiou, a manifestation of the "political and ethical paralysis" of contemporary neo-liberal capitalism, characterised by a cynical undermining of "the legitimacy of any cultural authority to curtail the freedoms of the sovereign individual" (Raymen, 2019: 136). Rejecting rights as providing a secure basis on which to found social harm, Raymen argues that zemiology needs a theory of the Good from which social harm is derived – and adds that "Pemberton has expressed this precise sentiment when he writes that 'we gain an understanding of harm exactly because it represents the converse reality of an imagined desirable state'" (Pemberton, 2015: 32).

Raymen uses Pemberton's reference to "human flourishing" – the capacity that harm disrupts and stunts – to insert Aristotle's idea of the telos of human life, which, following MacIntyre and others, he argues "could provide the objective reference point that can not only resolve moral or zemiological disagreements, but also offer guidance as to how to live the Good life" (Raymen, 2019: 149). This requires thorough, collective deliberation "about the common human good and the kinds of subjectivities, virtues and institutional values that are required for its achievement … within the communities to which we belong" (Raymen, 2019: 148–149). These communities themselves are the sites of the social practices, social roles and their institutions through which MacIntryre argues we strive towards the Good.

Without a theory of the Good – an appetite for grand ideological causes or the ability to imagine transformative visions of society based upon a new politics, economics or ethics, both precluded by neo-liberal capitalism – we cannot establish any clear consensus around social harm. For Raymen, harm is defined by deviation from or denial of the overall good by first of all pursuing the shared goods that are internal to social practices which themselves constitute the Good society. 'Zemiologists' must cease reformist work around piecemeal 'harm-minimisation' where social harms are risks to be managed. Rather, they must challenge the assumptions of liberalism and the needs of capital to take on the "deep but ultimately solvable social problems" these produce (Raymen, 2019: 145). In this fundamental challenge to zemiology, however, is also some endorsement of the current approach taken by some of its proponents. Raymen concludes thus:

> Within such writings, there is a broad tendency to develop typologies of harmful outcomes; be it physical harms, emotional harms, workplace harms, financial harms, environmental harms and so on ... As the name suggests, the obvious purpose of these typologies is to document the various types of harm scholars are interested in. However, I would suggest that there is something more significant taking place here. What all of these typologies are doing is locating and organising harms as they take place within specific spaces, places and social fields. I would like to surmise that, perhaps subconsciously and without necessarily realising the full philosophical implications of doing so, what they all implicitly suggest is that the question of ethics and what constitutes social harm is to be found through the exploration of social practices. They suggest that something has gone wrong with this social practice, which, by extension, suggests that there exists some Good or internal telos of these practices from which they have diverged. Indeed, Hillyard and Tombs have come closest to this sentiment when they write that social harm is defined, in part, by its operationalization and how it is deployed in practice upon social fields.
>
> *(Raymen, 2019: 157)*

It is clear then, even on the basis of this brief review, that there is no consensus on the essence of social harm, and in this sense there remains significant conceptual work to be done. However, again on the basis of this brief review, several tentative conclusions can be drawn as to the state of play of the concept:

- There is some agreement that social harm is related to the denial of human needs, albeit that there is no simple theory of needs by which these, or the harmful denial of them, can be recognised.
- Human beings have the capacities towards flourishing and self-realisation, and fulfilling such capacities is intrinsic to being human – so that harm is identified as the absence or stunting of such self-actualisation.
- Self-actualisation and human flourishing requires a good society, and that good society is one which must be envisioned, imagined and brought

BOX 4.5 AUTHOR'S NOTE: EXPERIENTIAL AND EPISTEMOLOGICAL LIMITATIONS – WHITENESS AND INSTITUTIONALISED RACISM IN CONTEMPORARY ZEMIOLOGY

As with almost every other aspect of the social sciences situated in the Global North, zemiology is significantly over-represented by white academics and activists. Indeed, across a still emerging discipline, there is a palpable lack of Black or minority ethnic collaborators. This matters for many reasons. First, it is itself an indicator that zemiology risks failing to address structural racism which is inherent to colonialities of power and thus the institutions and organisations within which we live and work. Second, it risks narrowing our sociological focus in ways which continue to white-wash knowledge. Experience – both lived and through grassroot movements – often gives us insight into social structures that others are not aware of. Consider, for example, that white people in most countries are less likely to be subject to police harassment, experience disproportionate imprisonment or subject to intersectional inequalities based on race or nationality with gender, ability and/or LGBTQI status. Such structural and institutional violence can become secondary to the focus of research or knowledge production, which is in itself harmful. Thus, it is the role of researchers and activists to establish and build meaningful links and research teams which reject dominant, white-centric practice.

Third, structural disempowerment of groups occurs through anti-Semitism, racism, sexism, Islamophobia and rising xenophobia. As such, it is often those who are subject to multiple barriers that go on to experience disproportionate levels of harm. On international scales, this can include state violence (Papua New Guinea), genocide (Myanmar), border harms (Manus Island and Nauru) – the list, and its casualties, goes on (see Gopal, 2019). As such it is important that the future of zemiology moves not towards surface-level representation, but a reinvigoration and gradual decolonisation of research agendas so that projects are led by or co-led by and with people who are most affected by social harms on endemic scales. With this said, we emphasise there is a fine balance between acting as allies to Black and minority ethnic zemiologists in a way that does not leave those most affected by harms to always have to research, deal with or address them, and continuing white-centric dominance of discourse by speaking on behalf of people, rather than with colleagues (Eddo-Lodge, 2018).

Lastly, as with survivors of Grenfell and survivors of sexual violence, it is important that researchers and activists work towards ensuring autonomy to both participate or not participate, both without pressure or coercion. The very point of social sciences, zemiology included, is that we can learn to understand aspects of the world around us. However, there is again a fine line between documenting, narrating and addressing social harm. The former two of these can have a tendency to lean toward voyeuristically relaying voice without context. Although they might form part of the bigger picture, zemiology should not confine itself to relaying painful or impactful stories and problems, but examine in depth the processes, structures and policies which produce them. This aspect will be discussed in further depth in the following chapter.

into being by men and women pursuing shared goods through social practices across a variety of social fields and institutions.

- That good society is certainly one that transcends forms of liberalism and capitalism, based upon rights, negative liberties and the proliferation of exchange values, one characterised by economic and cultural justice. In its absence, more or less social harm will remain.

Conclusion

In the preceding chapters we have considered – and sought to clarify – the different ways that social harm and zemiology might be viewed, determined, defined. We have seen that once we move away from discourses of 'crime', including the harms that people may face as an effect of social control or the lack of it, there are some clear and increasingly agreed upon ways to think about harm as something that is likely to affect all of us throughout our lives.

In the previous chapter we outlined a typology of harms which can help us do this: from physical harms to harms of recognition, we can perceive how and where people have detrimental social experiences that might otherwise be avoided or mitigated. We have sought in this chapter to further outline the relations aspects of harm, how harms work and the basis upon which we can identify harms as harms. Most fundamentally, if still unapologetically tentatively, we identify harms as those actions, omissions, policies, processes, conditions, states of affairs, assumptions, ways of doing things and dominant structures which contribute to the absence of or distortions in self-actualisation.

At this point, we will now move to think about how exactly we can approach and research harm from a zemiological perspective. What approaches or concepts might be helpful? What questions should we ask to gain knowledge that might harvest alternative insights into harm in the everyday? And how might we go about developing research projects which help us gain meaningful insight in ways that lead us to further understand the mechanisms of social harm, and how it might be mitigated or eradicated? In short, how can we *do* zemiology?

References

Bhatia, M. and Canning, V. (2021) Introduction, in *Stealing Time: Migration Contested Temporalities and State Violence*, edited by V. Canning, M. Bhatia, and S. Khosravi, Basingstoke: Palgrave Macmillan.

Bhopal, K. (2018) *White Privilege: The Myth of a Post-Racial Society*, Bristol: Policy.

Black Lives Matter (2020a) *Black Lives Matter Global Network Responses to COVID-19 Ethnicity Data*, 9 April, https://blacklivesmatter.com/black-lives-matter-global-network-responses-to-covid-19-ethnicity-data/ (Accessed 14 August 2020).

Black Lives Matter (2020b) *#DefundThePolice*, 30 May, https://blacklivesmatter.com/defundthepolice/ (Accessed 14 August 2020).

Black Lives Matter (n.d.) *About*, https://blacklivesmatter.com/about/ (Accessed 14 August 2020).

Booth, R. and Barr, C. (2020) Black people four times more likely to die from Covid-19, ONS finds, *The Guardian*, 7 May, www.theguardian.com/world/2020/may/07/black-people-four-times-more-likely-to-die-from-covid-19-ons-finds (Accessed 18 August 2020).

Cain, M. and Howe, A. (2008) *Women, Crime and Social Harm: Towards a Criminology for the Global Era*, Portland: Hart Publishing.

Canning, V. (2017) *Gendered Harm and Structural Violence in the British Asylum System*, Oxon: Routledge.

Canning, V. (2018) Zemiology at the border, in *Zemiology: Reconnecting Crime and Social Harm*, edited by A. Boukli and J. Kotzé, Basingstoke: Palgrave Macmillan, 183–203.

Cole, M. (2020) Criminology, harm and non-human animals, in *Crime, Harm and the State. Book 1*, edited by L. Copson, E. Dimou and S. Tombs, Milton Keynes: Open University Press, 111–143.

Copson, L. (2011) *Archaeologies of Harm: Criminology, Critical Criminology, Zemiology*. Unpublished PhD Thesis, Faculty of Social Sciences and Law, School of Sociology, University of Bristol.

Cruelty Free International (n.d.) *Facts and Figures on Animal Testing*, www.crueltyfreeinternational.org/why-we-do-it/facts-and-figures-animal-testing (Accessed 14 August 2020).

Davis, A. Y. (2008) *Are Prisons Obsolete?*, New York: Seven Stories Press.

Doyal, L. (1993) Thinking about human need, *New Left Review*, I (201), 113–128.

Doyal, L. and Gough, I. (1991) *A Theory of Human Need*, Basingstoke: Palgrave Macmillan.

Eddo-Lodge, R. (2018) *Why I'm No Longer Talking to White People About Race*, London: Bloomsbury.

Evans, K. (2019) Ancient farmers burned the Amazon, but today's fires are very different, *National Geographic*, www.nationalgeographic.com/environment/2019/09/ancient-humans-burned-amazon-fires-today-entirely-different/ (Accessed 19 June 2020).

Fraser, N. (2000) Rethinking recognition, *New Left Review*, 3, 107–120.

Garside, R. (2013) Addressing social harm: Better regulation versus social transformation, *Revista Crítica Penal y Poder*, 5, 247–265.

Gopal, P. (2019) *Insurgent Empire: Anti-colonial Resistance and British Dissent*, London: Verso Books.

Goyes, D. R. (2019) *A Southern Green Criminology: Science Against Ecological Discrimination*, Bingley: Emerald.

Hall, S. and Winlow, S. (2018) Big trouble or little evils: The ideological struggle over the concept of harm, in *Zemiology: Reconnecting Crime and Social Harm*, edited by A. Boukli and J. Kotzé, Switzerland: Palgrave Macmillan, 107–126.

Hillyard, P. and Tombs, S. (2004) Towards a political economy of harm: States, corporations and the production of inequality, in *Beyond Criminology? Taking Harm Seriously*, edited by P. Hillyard, C. Pantazis, S. Tombs and D. Gordon, London: Pluto Press, 30–54.

Iliadou, E. (2019) *Border Harms and Everyday Violence: The Lived Experiences of Border Crossers in Lesvos Island, Greece*, PhD Thesis in Criminology and Social Policy, Open University, January.

Large, J. (2018) Spot the fashion victim(s): The importance of rethinking harm within the context of fashion counterfeiting, in *Zemiology: Reconnecting Crime and Social Harm*, edited by A. Boukli and J. Kotzé, Basingstoke: Palgrave Macmillan, 223–245.

Lasslett, K. (2010) Crime or social harm? A dialectical perspective, *Crime, Law and Social Change*, 54, 1–19.

Leonardo, Z. (2009) *Race, Whiteness and Education*, London and New York: Routledge.

Mitchell, D., Pantazis, C. and Pemberton, S., eds. (2019) Culture, consumption and social harm. Special Issue of *Justice, Power and Resistance*, 3 (2).

Pantazis, C. and Pemberton, S. (2009) Nation states and the production of social harm: Resisting the hegemony of 'TINA', in *State, Crime, Power*, edited by R. Coleman, J. Sim, S. Tombs and D. Whyte, London: Sage, 214–233.

Pantazis, C., Pemberton, S. and Mitchell, D., eds. (2019) Neo-liberalism and harm production. Special Issue of *Justice, Power and Resistance*, 3 (1).

Peggs, K. (2012) *Animals and Sociology*, Basingstoke: Palgrave Macmillan.

Pemberton, S. (2007) Social harm future(s): Exploring the potential of the social harm approach, *Crime, Law and Social Change*, 48, 27–41.
Pemberton, S. (2015) *Harmful Societies: Understanding Social Harm*, Bristol: Policy Press.
Ramaswamy, C. (2017) Trayvon Martin's parents, five years on: 'Racism is alive and well in America', *The Guardian*, 13 February, www.theguardian.com/us-news/2017/feb/13/trayvon-martin-parents-racism-alive-and-well-in-america (Accessed 14 August 2020).
Raymen, T. (2019) The enigma of social harm and the barrier of liberalism: Why zemiology needs a theory of the Good, *Justice, Power and Resistance*, 3 (1), 134–163.
Smith, A. (2015) *Conquest: Sexual Violence and American Indian Genocide*, USA: Duke University Press.
Soliman, F. (2019) States of exception, human rights and social harm: Towards a border zemiology, *Theoretical Criminology*, online first: 1–19.
Sollund, R. (2012) Oil production, climate change and species decline: The case of Norway, in *Climate Change from a Criminological Perspective*, edited by R. White, New York: Springer, 135–147.
Sollund, R., ed. (2015) *Green Harms and Crimes: Critical Criminology in a Changing World*, Basingstoke: Palgrave Macmillan.
Soper, K. (1993) A theory of human need, *New Left Review*, 1 (197), 113–128.
South, N. and Brisman, A. (2013) Introduction, in *The Routledge International Handbook of Green Criminology*, edited by N. South and A. Brisman, New York: Routledge, 1–23.
Tombs, S. (2015) Harmful societies, *Criminal Justice Matters*, 101, 36–37.
Tombs, S. (2020) Crime and harm in the food industry, in *Crime, Harm and the State. Book 1*, edited by L. Copson, E. Dimou and S. Tombs, Milton Keynes: Open University Press, 1215–249.
Tombs, S. and Whyte, D. (2015) *The Corporate Criminal: Why Corporations Must Be Abolished*, Oxon: Routledge.
Vanguard (2018) *Inside Ogoni Village Where Oil Spill 'Wipes off 10 People Every Week'*, www.vanguardngr.com/2018/12/inside-ogoni-village-where-oil-spill-wipes-off-10-persons-every-week/ (Accessed 19 June 2020).
Walters, R. (2011) *Eco Crime and Genetically Modified Food*, New York: Routledge.
Walters, R. (2018) Climate change denial: Making ignorance great again, in *Ignorance, Power and Harm: Agnotology and the Criminological Imagination*, edited by A. Barton and H. Davis, Basingstoke: Palgrave Macmillan, 163–187.
White, R. (2018) *Climate Change Criminology*, Bristol: Bristol University Press.
Whyte, D. (2020) *Ecocide: Kill the Corporation Before It Kills Us*, Manchester: Manchester University Press.
Wyatt, T. (2013) *Wildlife Trafficking: A Deconstruction of the Crime, the Victims, and the Offenders*, Basingstoke: Palgrave Macmillan.
Yar, M. (2012) Critical criminology, critical theory and social harm, in *New Directions in Criminological Theory*, edited by S. Hall and S. Winlow, London: Routledge, 52–65.

5
DOING ZEMIOLOGY

Introduction

In the two previous chapters we sought to develop our understanding of the conceptual terrain of social harm, and what this means for a zemiology based upon this terrain. In this chapter we turn our attention to consider how to further 'know' about harms in ways that might contribute ultimately to counteracting or mitigating those harms. In short, we offer some preliminary observations on what it is to 'do' zemiology. Intrinsic to doing zemiology is understanding a wide gamut of harmful policies, practices and processes, with explicit commitments to recognising and confronting inequality, poverty, injustice or social control and thus furthering social justice.

Researching social harm often involves doing at least one of two things: exposing, documenting, mapping and understanding a harm or harms as they have been experienced *and* how they have been produced. In this chapter we shall make some zemiological observations on these two – inter-related, of course – activities – and then consider what they imply for counter-hegemonic practices.

What might zemiologists research?

Zemiology aims to maintain and extend a focus on harms that are almost so large, common, routine that we often fail to see them – industrial-scale harms, operating at structural and institutional levels – whilst still recognising the importance of the individual experiences when people are affected by harm. As we have indicated, such research has included harms and/or death at work (Lloyd, 2018; Tombs and Whyte, 2017), female genital mutilation (Karlsen *et al.*, 2019), border harms (Canning, 2017, 2018; Soliman, 2019), the harms of 'fast fashion' (Large, 2018; Simončič, 2017) and environmental harm (Walters, 2018; White, 2018).

Thus zemiology, studying social harm, requires a rethink about the lens through which we view the world in which we live. As the above indicates, the kinds of harms upon which zemiology focuses may not, indeed rarely, fall into the 'shock factor' category that brutal murders or abuse exposés might understandably draw. Rather they often go unseen or are so deeply embedded in everyday lives that the extent of their harms becomes normalised and thus overlooked. Indeed, harm can be embedded in something as seemingly uncontroversial as getting dressed.

As introduced in Chapter 2, Large outlines that what many of us wear on any given day is likely to have been produced as part of a trajectory of variable dimensions and sites of harm (2018). Mass production of clothing garments is the product of globalised industries which centralise corporate capital. As such, almost all aspects of mass-produced fashion relate to harm: from the use of Indigenous land for cotton production to the privatization of water to facilitate its growth. Caste and class-based harms are gendered and racialised in terms of exploitation of labour, often in dire and unsafe working conditions akin to factory farms. On scratching the surface, the human costs of such conditions have capacity to inflict or compound economic, physical or psychological harms, further impacted by gendered roles and class and caste inequalities. Dig even further and we can begin to consider the ecological and environmental harms inherent to the process: the privatisation and/or redistribution of water, often in hot countries in the Global South which are most affected by drought, affects humans and non-humans like (Bick *et al.*, 2018). Moreover, when we consider the amount of transport required to move clothing across the globe, we shift into the realm of pollution, environmental harm and even negative impacts of dumped goods on land and in the world's oceans. In short, a zemiological lens can highlight harms that are part of everyday aspects of life across the globe, even things that seem as banal as putting on clothes – for those working in the mass production of clothing – getting up and going to work.

Adopting a social harm perspective or a zemiological framework in fact opens up a mass of research topics which affect people's everyday life experiences across the globe on a daily basis whether they recognise that fact or not. Of course, what these topics are and how we approach them depends upon our disciplinary expertise. Differing disciplinary backgrounds means engaging in a zemiology with a focus upon different clusters of harms. For example, within the context of political economy there have recently been efforts to uncover the harmful consequences of the privileging of home ownership (Schelhase, 2020) and distinct economies with distinct institutions, rules and practices (DeMartino, 2019). Across medicine, concerned with all forms of physical and mental health, there are concerns with iatrogenic harm – 'doctor-originating' harm, generated by medical practice, whether legally negligent or not, and thus breaking "the oldest and most famous rule of medical ethics: *primum non nocere*, or above all, do no harm" (Klaas *et al.*, 2014: 1279).

Table 5.1 shows a set of issues covered in a module based in a UK university which traverses criminology, social harm and zemiology.[1] In the left-hand column are the broad areas addressed in teaching weeks, and in the right-hand column are a set of prescribed topic areas upon which students could choose to undertake their own independent study.

It is worth drawing out some observations on this table. First, this is, in many respects, a random set of areas. But it is not *wholly* random in the sense that, while it might have been constructed very differently, there are logics as to what does and can appear here. As stated, these areas and topics are drawn from a module in a Department which spans criminology, social harm and zemiology. We both work in and around critical criminology. This book is part of a series focusing on 'New Directions in Critical Criminology'. It is inevitable, therefore, those issues where we do zemiology will have some *proximity* to 'crime', criminal justice and non/criminalisation – however, we reiterate, as in earlier chapters, that zemiology remains peripheral to, but not under, this disciplinary umbrella.

Second, as a set of areas with some proximity to 'crime' and critical criminology, it covers a host of areas of social life which might be subject to zemiological enquiry – including some of those referred to in this book or already the subject of zemiological research such as excess winter deaths, housing policy and financial crises.

Third, it is clear that, while some of the broad areas and the more focused topics are related to each other, perhaps over-lap, and that there could be movement within these, there is also enormous scope for developing these topics. For example, and quite clearly, the topic areas identifying harms relating to gender and racial identities or to non-human animals could both be significantly expanded. The focus on the food industry could be extended to similar study on virtually any industry of any significance. In other words, even for a set of considerations that relate to crime and criminology, as do those in Table 5.1, this table illustrates the vast range of possibilities that fall within zemiology, possibilities which, too, remain consistent with a concept

TABLE 5.1 Areas for potential and further zemiological study

Broad Area of Study	*More Focussed Topic*
The harms of regulation	• Gambling • Pornography • Precarious employment • Routine corporate violence
The harms of criminalisation	• The war on drugs • The overrepresentation of minorities in justice systems • Subsided private corporate profits • The governance of 'disengaged' young people
The harms of legal drugs	• Tobacco • Alcohol • The transatlantic trade in sugar • Pharmaceuticals and pharmaharms
Harm to non-human animals	• Horse-racing • 'Livestock' farming • Fishing • The trade in 'rare species'
Harms relating to gender and racial identities	• Legal regulation of sexuality • State and perpetuation gendered roles • Skin lightening • Advertising
Neo-colonial harms	• Trade in conflict minerals • Tourism • Racism • Global inequalities
Harms associated with the food industry	• Fast/junk food • Avocado production in the South • Access to potable water • Fairtrade
State-inflicted harms	• Deaths in care homes • Deaths in custody • The 'war on terror' • Global pandemics
Harms and border controls	• The refugee 'crisis' • Points-based immigration systems • 'Crimmigration' • Far-right groups

TABLE 5.1 Cont.

Broad Area of Study	*More Focussed Topic*
Harms and surveillance	• Border controls and security practices • Identification technologies • CCTV • Cybercrime
Harms and armed conflict	• The global arms trade • Private military companies • Genocide • Civil warfare
'Green' harms	• Ecocide • Climate catastrophe • The overexploitation of resources • Exposure to deadly pollutants

of social harm which, albeit nascent and still be to be fully formed, is consistent with the discussion in Chapters 3 and 4.

All in all, zemiology marks out a rich, diverse area for research.

Having indicated what is entailed in doing zemiology – those kinds of areas, issues, questions which it might address – we turn to consider some aspects of how we do zemiology. We begin these considerations by addressing zemiological discourse, and in particular some of the relationships between language and knowledge claims within a zemiological framework.

Language and knowledge claims

In doing zemiology, we should place significant emphasis on how language is used and exercised. As Foucault highlighted, discourse, not least language and linguistic terms, is saturated in power: the power to name, to produce or use certain words, or influence what we know or prioritise as knowledge (Du Bois, 1898; Foucault, 1972, 1977). Moreover, that which becomes named and known often becomes seen or misconstrued as 'truth'. Historically this very issue has caused untold harms, particularly within criminology, medicine and psychiatry which based many earlier beliefs – and subsequently practices – on biological and psychological notions of deviance, pain and illness. In other words, the power of disciplinary language enabled the perpetuation of assumptions of certain groups in society, such as people women deemed 'hysterical' or people living with disabilities deemed 'monstrous', and justified invasive and violent physical and psychological experiments.

When researching from a zemiological perspective, it's important to carefully consider words which already carry specific historical and current understandings. For example, the word crime immediately makes us think about an individual who breaks the law. An image of a group of suited men sitting around a table and deciding to pollute the water supply to save costs to their company, does not enter our consciousness. Similarly, we do not think about the changes to social security, which directly caused people to die or end their own lives. The word also narrows our response to the incident or behaviour. We are forced to think about arrest, prosecution conviction and, crucially, punishment. All the words which are derived from crime, such as criminal, criminalisation, criminality, criminogenic, crimination, criminology and criminologist all force thinking in a selective direction. In order to think about harm, we need to use terms which do not carry specific histories and meanings, nor imply particular types of responses to them. If we are to move beyond the traditional and failed response to harmful acts we need to stop using the word crime and all words derived from it, or associated with it. Care should also be taken with the concept of 'criminal justice'. The word justice assumes some quality of being just, of impartiality or fairness. The word justice raises expectations that it will be achieved, but seldom is and distorts the reality of what actually takes place. In short, we need to be imaginative and think of new words to cover the harmful behaviour.

But this is not simply a case of avoiding certain terms, it is also a case of extending the use of others. There have long been struggles to attach the label violence to certain phenomena in order to change the social seriousness with which they are viewed – and, perhaps, subsequently responded to. These include:

- the (successful) campaigning and academic work of feminists to attach the label of violence to some forms of inter-personal encounters within inter-personal relationships and households – the latter becoming known as domestic and sexual violence;
- the development of the concepts of institutional and structural violence, outlined in Chapter 2;
- the re-identification of 'accidents' and 'disasters' related to workplaces from trains to oil installations to garment factories as instances of corporate violence or corporate killing;

- the ascription of the term social murder – introduced and defined via Engels in Chapter 3 – to the joint actions and omissions of a range of corporate and state bodies which produced what otherwise might be referred to as the Grenfell Tower fire or tragedy.

So, altering language has the potential to provide different understandings of harmful events. Consider for example an act which from a criminological perspective is called a 'burglary' defined in terms of a 'criminal breaking in' to a house, throwing everything out of drawers and 'stealing' £200, leaving credit cards and passports. The emotional response to this 'criminal' act may be a sense of violation, fear and a reaction that whomever is responsible for it should be punished. From a zemiological perspective, the same event can be reconstituted in a very different way. Rather than defining the event as a 'crime' it is seen as a failure of someone to adequately secure the house, an act of desperation or survival by an individual, and the 'theft' as an act of redistribution. Then the understanding and emotional response to the same act may be very different. Negative emotions are replaced by more positive thoughts of empathy. A focus on the wrongs of the individual might be subsumed within more general considerations of their wider circumstances, institutions and structures. Instead of wishing that the person is punished by the state, the state becomes an object of critical scrutiny for its failures to ensure full economic, political and social citizenship to such individuals. At the same time, this may generate compassion towards the unknown individual and a concern about their survival.

Now, of course, we do not pretend that any of these shifts are easy, or undermine the feelings we may experience having been subjected to wrongdoing, but a precondition of any of them is moving from the discourse of individualised criminality, crime, wrongdoing, punishment, and so on. And part of this discursive shift is about the language we use to speak and think. These are the prerequisites that allow us to at least begin to make moves towards building an alternative form of collective consciousness that might help us better respond to problems when they arise without resorting to penalty and retributive 'justice' as a first means of response (see Malloch, 2016; Mathiesen and Hjemdal, 2016).

Likewise, as zemiology develops there should be collective care taken in prioritising language which does not 'other' in ways that remove agency or objectify suffering. As critical race theorists and anti-colonialist scholars have long noted, there has been a tendency for academic research and writing to talk 'about', for example, Black experiences of social injustice in ways which perpetuate stereotypes of dependency and vulnerability. Thus references to the Black 'attainment gap' in, for example, schools or higher education, do not just focus attention upon the 'achievements' or otherwise of Black and Asian heritage students but it positively obscures from view the structures of power within which those 'achievements' can only be understood through the historical and contemporaneous dimensions of white privilege which maintains and benefits from these. The objective of zemiological language should be to focus on the processes of powers which create and sustain the sites and dimensions of harm outlined in the previous chapter, therefore opening more ways to consider how these harms can be resisted.

Terms of speech are particularly important as they can undermine or even deny dignity and humanity. From a zemiological perspective, it is imperative that legalistic notions or definitions which 'other' people are not used to denote individuals or groups, and we should refrain from assigning statuses and reducing identities through the use of terms based in legal frameworks. Take people who have been in prison as an example. Such a person may be a friend, a postal worker or doctor, a partner, sibling, parent or carer. However, for a period of time they may be referred to as a 'prisoner', an 'illegal immigrant' or an 'offender'. Their overall identity is stripped, replaced only by a temporal legal status or a successfully processed claim regarding a legal transgression rather than any holistic notion of that person. Moreover, for people convicted of offences, this status becomes fixed to the identity long after release, where people might be termed 'ex-offender' or 'ex-prisoner' indefinitely.

Further extending this focus on the significance of language, Cole has recently discussed the 'animal turn' in the social sciences. His starting point is to jar the usual distinction as separate categories those beings indicated by the terms 'humans' and 'animals'. This obscures the fact that "humans are also 'animals', of the species *homo sapiens* (Latin for 'knowing man')" (Cole, 2020: 117). Phrases like 'other animals', 'non-human animals' and 'animals other than humans' represent a deliberate ploy, designed to jar familiar linguistic terminology and to force us to pause to consider what we otherwise take for granted. Broadly, therefore, and crucially opened up through questioning discourse – language, representation and imagery – Cole focuses upon the 'animal turn', an increased attention across the social sciences to interconnections between humans and other animals, to facilitate "an increased *critical* focus on how human-nonhuman interconnections are riven with inequalities and can produce harms" (Cole, 2020: 115).

There is seldom sympathy for people who have committed violent offences – after all, if a person inflicts harm on another why should there be? To this we point again to the structural: once we dehumanise people by reducing them merely to legalistic terms and categories, it becomes easier to remove rights or broader civil liberties for all affected. It also creates systemic ideologies of 'us' and 'them', and people who are criminalised become 'othered'. This is despite the fact that many individuals in societies have committed illegalised acts or transgressed laws in one way or another, but have not been criminalised or imprisoned. Indeed, given that most people in prison come from poor backgrounds, are disproportionately affected by mental health problems and have disproportionately lived as cared-for children (Prison Reform Trust, 2019), the use of terms such as 'prisoner' or 'offender' can become confined to those who are less powerful in society. Whilst those inflicting harm on mass scales such as in governments are seldom associated with the terms 'prisoner' or 'offender', we are socially conditioned to train our attention on the deviant other, on 'crimes' of the powerless rather than endemic harms of the powerful.

In discussing these points in various public forums, we have been reminded that some people refer to themselves as 'prisoner' or 'offender'. Indeed, many do – including some of our friends or students who have been in prison. This is for many reasons: to own one's history, to accept wrong-doing or, for some, as a badge of honour or cultural capital. We do not question the right for individuals to self-identify in this way, but we do encourage critical discussion on how or why such terms have become some of the only avenues to express identity. Being in prison is – for most people – a short-term temporal experience. On release, people are often dubbed 'ex-offender' or 'ex-prisoner', suggesting these identities transgress all other parts of a person's history or personality. To move towards radical systematic change, we argue it is necessary to step away from the application of legally ascribed terms as actual lived identities, and concentrate instead on the human aspects of individuals in society.

Some principles of zemiological investigation

Further dimensions of how we 'do' zemiology relate to the ethics, politics and practices of zemiological inquiry: how we accumulate knowledge-claims should always be reflexively and carefully considered. Research in the social sciences is often, ostensibly at least, highly regulated and monitored. Researchers have to address many ethical issues to have projects approved before undertaking any empirical research, with a formal ethics approval process to be successfully navigated – albeit this often feels like a process whereby institutions weigh up the potential risk to their own corporate entity, perhaps reputationally if someone were to claim that information had been unethically obtained, or financially if compensable harm came to the researcher. Professional associations also issues ethical codes of practice, such as, for example, those generated by the British Sociological Association (British Sociological Association, 2017).

Ethics, harm, politics

Zemiological research should of course proceed ethically. But this is not the same as saying that it should adhere to existent, dominant understandings of what that means. For us, zemiology should strive to develop an alternate ethics, consistent with its ontological bases as to what it means to be harmed. This would be one which seeks to support research participants – those who are more likely to be or have been harmed – and at the same time seek to generate research which contributes to counter-hegemonic struggle, that is to disrupt the powerful. This starting point already reveals some key questions that the zemiological researchers should be asking, such as those indicated in Table 5.2.

The basic and most fundamental requirement here is to access the experiences of, and where possible to work with to support, those who have been subject to acute or chronic, ongoing harms. Of course, in identifying how to meet these aims we do not need to reinvent the wheel – there is much critical social science upon which to draw.

Thus, for example, a variety of feminist methodologies have long found ways to engage in research which aims to be non-exploitative and non-harmful with those who have been harmed both acutely and chronically. This can include longer-term engagements with people within organisations, and methods which require sustained and interactive engagement such as critical ethnographies, oral histories, activist participation and innovative or arts-based interventions.

As Victoria found when undertaking focus groups with women seeking asylum about maternity care (with Dr Helen Churchill), women often engaged with more discussion than expected and disclosed personal medical harms that helped un-silence some problems that otherwise may not be easy to discuss. It also allowed for women to recognise that they were not alone in their experience, so can also be a form of emancipatory consciousness-raising – a key aspect of feminist methodologies. This not only leads to researchers and activists better understanding how people experience personal problems, but also allow structural problems to be challenged through conversation. As such, using conversation – as well as other, more innovative forms of engagement (see Box 5.1) – to distribute information that may support in mitigating harms can be done in a similar way.

TABLE 5.2 Considerations for harm mitigation during research

Does the project have potential to cause further harm to participants?	Whilst some harms can be reduced, there may be times when certain groups might be negatively affected by engaging in empirical research without gaining much back. In some instances, it may be worth considering if a project truly requires first-hand narratives, or if critical information can already be gleaned from secondary sources.
Is there a clear objective to reduce or mitigate certain harmful practices or institutions?	Zemiology holds one fundamental objective as contributing to social change which may reduce harm. In some cases, this may simply be the act of documenting harms so that they can be recognised, exposed and named – not least for or on behalf of counter-hegemonic organisations. For others, this may mean engaging in longer-term projects pertaining to social change through activism, critical policy recommendations or taking part in or supporting longer-term social movements.
Are there ways to develop strategies to 'study up'?	This is one of the key facets of zemiology: understanding how powerful institutions, agencies, states and corporations work to produce and often simultaneously obscure harms. As such, although we may wish to focus on or work with people, groups or non-human animals to investigate the impacts of harms, this must always be accompanied, where feasible, with fore-grounding ways to critically scrutinise macro-level power. This relates to 'studying up', on which more below.

Of course, many of these same considerations would apply to others who might be deemed especially 'vulnerable'. Although for some, for example young people or people legally deemed as 'minors', there might additionally be required further specific legal consultations on accessing or including such groups, particularly if researching harm (such as experiencing or indeed inflicting harm). For this it may be useful to consider frameworks such as those set by the National Society for the Prevention of Cruelty to Children or other national and international guidance.

In general, a key issue is that working with those who have been harmed always runs the risk of generating further traumatisation.

BOX 5.1 CASE STUDY EXAMPLE BY VICTORIA: THE RIGHT TO REMAIN ASYLUM NAVIGATION BOARD

The *Right to Remain Asylum Navigation Board,* was developed in 2018 by myself and Lisa Matthews. Just before summer of that year, sitting on the floor of a room in the North West of England, Ala (pseudonym) was showing scars on her arms from where her husband had burned her. It was not the first time a woman has shown me such scars, and it is unlikely to be the last. But beyond the pains evident on her body, one curious sentence struck a chord when she was speaking of her refusal for refugee status: "I didn't give the right papers. I'm just no good".

For some years, Lisa (coordinator at *Right to Remain*) and I have listened separately to people whose claims to asylum in the UK are refused and who blame themselves for their refusal. From entering the UK until decision or appeal, significant pressure is placed on individuals to 'prove' they are persecuted enough (and in the 'right way') to be considered a refugee. The cuts to legal aid and the introduction of measures to make it more difficult to access justice, such as changes to judicial review stopping forced removal and the introduction of 'removal windows' have made the asylum process ever more complicated and difficult to navigate successfully. We have often watched as people with little or no legal knowledge or training are expected to put together their own cases for appeals, as solicitors are ever stretched and support increasingly squeezed. The increased price of legal representation means some people – receiving less than £40 per week – are expected to cover their own legal costs. As I have written elsewhere, for some, this has meant making decisions between eating sufficient quality or amounts of food, or saving to fund their case. For others, this facilitates exploitative illegal work, which for women is disproportionately sexualised in nature.

There is no easy way to solve the problems faced by Ala and so many others. The now well-recognised 'hostile environment' orchestrated by the British state and often enacted by its corporate allies has been developed specifically to facilitate deterrence and deportation. As such, any remedy or resistance requires complex and sustained intervention in the long run.

It is at this intersection that Lisa and I opted for a short-term intervention to support the rights of people seeking asylum. How can we collectively ensure that people obtain accurate information in a way that enables a recognition that this is a system built to make gaining asylum difficult? With legal advice at its most sparse and prices for representation increasing, there are ever more ways for inaccurate information to drip through to people who are newly arrived and do not understand each step of the asylum process. Moreover, considering that inaccurate information can have devastating effects for a person's claim to asylum, how do we enable correct information to be distributed from the offset?

It was from this starting point that the *Right to Remain* asylum navigation board has developed. The board acts as two things: first, it is a pedagogic tool for facilitators working with people seeking asylum (including people who have themselves been through the process) to outline each step of the system. Information cards align with colours, and the *Right to Remain* toolkit acts as a further guide for each stage. From there, each colour on the board aligns with cards highlighting potential problems and solutions.

Second – and central to the political importance of consciousness raising discussed above – the board aims to work as a consciousness-raising tool. The words uttered by Ala, "I'm just no good" are a manifestation of the individualising, dehumanising effects of the process of seeking asylum for many of the people who go through it. By bringing

> people together who have similar experiences, the board is a vehicle for discussion, mutual aid and collective recognition of the endemic issues embedded in the system itself. So often, we have seen the power of collectivity in the groups and friendships we have been involved with – when together, and with an opportunity to talk through the problems faced and solutions sought, there is more scope to de-individualise the issues so deeply embedded in the legal and formal process of seeking asylum in the UK.
>
> Adapted from Canning and Matthews (2018)

It is clear that there are fine lines between avoiding the potential for causing further harm and excavating experiences and narratives of harm. It is equally clear that there are some contexts where people have been so recently or significantly affected by specific events resulting in harm that those directly affected should not be approached. This means that research is simply not done unless at the explicit and fully informed invitation of those affected groups most affected by harm. Nor does it mean that research cannot be undertaken in ways which do not involve the direct participation of those harmed but which maintains the experiences of those at its centre. One example of the latter is to be found in research conducted in the aftermath of the Grenfell Tower fire in London, in June 2017, as outlined in the introduction chapter.

Mitigating harm for researchers

These considerations only start to scratch the surface of the ethics and politics of researching and working with those harmed. Nor do they address the potential harm involved in such work for those undertaking zemiology. So there is a further, harm-related question to be asked prior to doing zemiology: what harms might researchers face and do they have the support to mitigate these both in the short-term and to ensure that they do not face longer-term harms?

All research projects or investigations should have outlets for discussion or raising concerns, as well as ensuring that people do not experience harms from research. If you are leading a zemiological research project, you should ensure to centralise support and opportunities for research breaks so that other researchers can reduce the likelihood of experiencing burn-out. If you are researching on behalf of an organisation or institution, ask what processes are in place to avoid (for example) vicarious trauma, and request that they be implemented from the offset.

Long-term engagement with social harm can lead to a range of problematic situations from vicarious trauma (that is, developing symptoms reflective of trauma such as sleeplessness, anxiety or depression) to burnout, where researchers (as with activists) can feel diminished, overly saddened or generally exhausted by feelings of saturation or – worse, hopelessness if social change and progress are not forthcoming. These are entirely comprehensible, common experiences which are to be expected, especially when researchers are emotionally invested in change or social justice. As feminist and pioneering Black rights activist Audre Lorde argued, self-care is a radical act if it enables us to continue to fight for social and structural change. Yet here the resources and contexts for such self-care that might be provided through institutions to facilitate, nurture, encourage zemiological research are precisely those resources most likely to continue to be eroded with the long march through the institutions of many Higher Education sectors on the part of the values and practices of marketisation, financialisation and neoliberalism, in the UK and in many other national contexts. Indeed, this is increasingly replaced with surface-level strategies that may equate to little more than 'some me time'. Structural changes that are required to ensure reasonable working conditions – such as being allocated enough time or workload hours, or being provided with emotional support and regular supervision – can become conflated with the provision of online wellbeing courses or the provision of yoga classes, amongst others. Of course this is not to say these are not necessarily positive or helpful, but rather they should be supplementary to (rather than in place of) acceptable research and teaching conditions.

Studying-up

There is one final dimension to researching harm which also needs to be highlighted – thinking about the needs and interests of those who have been harmed is the flip side of considering who or what is doing the harming. And this latter consideration is crucial if we are to fully address the aim of research which exposes such harms, potentially mitigates them or leads to harm reduction and prevention.

In this context, it is worth noting that Alvesalo-Kuusi and Whyte (2018) have taken some of the key elements which generally appear in professional codes of ethics statements, and reappraised them in the light of researching the powerful. They set out these generic core principles as follows:

> *the harm principle*, where steps must be taken to minimise 'harm' (normally referring to psychological or physical harm to participants);

> researchers should guard against the *invasion of privacy*, so that anonymity and confidentiality guarantees are given either unconditionally, or sometimes on request, as a prerequisite of research;
>
> the *prevention of deception*, whereby the researcher must avoid deceiving the research participant;
>
> to minimise deception, researchers apply the related principle of *informed consent* where research subjects are given as much knowledge about the research as is necessary to allow them to make an informed decision about their participation.
>
> (2018: 141)

Now on one level – and as researchers are accustomed to internalise through their professional training, and as is reinforced by every ethics application for any one research project – these seem entirely reasonable, perhaps axiomatic, principles of social research. Alvesalo-Kuusi and Whyte critique these principles in some depth, particularly in the context of researching crimes or harms of the powerful (see Box 5.2). Importantly, they highlight that ethics frameworks as they are often currently formulated do not fully take into account structural dynamics of power, in their case in the context of corporate crime and harm. Such principles in fact assume that research is to be carried out on the relatively powerless. But Alvesalo-Kuusi and Whyte invert them in exposing the barriers in accessing and researching powerful actors and institutions, and so argue that research ethics as they currently stand is a key obstacle to piercing the protections which the powerful erect for themselves to evade critical scrutiny, such protections being one of the defining aspects of power.

Thus, more broadly, Alvesalo-Kuusi and Whyte argue that standards for codes and ethics are developed from agendas often founded in liberal higher institutions which place normative forms of impact – such as policy recommendations – at the fore of their outcome objectives. Importantly, this does not reflect the ideals of radical research or indeed support the makings of research which aims to study those who are most powerful in and across societies. Instead they call for a reconstruction of social science research ethics based on a collectivist understanding of the 'public interest' that is not exclusively defined for and by the academy but connects to all groups interested in knowing about the closed-off worlds of the powerful (2018: 136). It is these kinds of considerations which must be taken into account as zemiology develops.

Here a final consideration should be noted. In whichever arena we wish to study harm, accessing people in powerful institutions can be incredibly complex. Funding can be difficult to obtain, and critical researchers should

BOX 5.2 WHAT IS MEANT BY 'THE POWERFUL'?

Defining power is no easy feat. For Marxist sociologists, power might be strongly associated with capital and the means of production. Foucauldian thinkers might consider that power uses pre-existing knowledge and reproduces this knowledge to further create or exercise power (such as through language, as discussed earlier). Critical race theorists and decolonialists highlight racialised aspects of power, particularly in terms of global capital, exploitation and racialised state violence (criminalisation included – see Patel and Tyrer, 2011). Many feminist scholars and activists place patriarchy in a central facet of power and links with gendered oppression (Emejulu and Sobande, 2019). Power can be multi-lateral, embedded in unequal macro or institutional structures, or weaved through inter-personal relationships in the everyday. In many ways, powers at both ends of this continuum can be connected.

As such, in developing research agendas, zemiology benefits from recognising the complexities of power: that individuals may have power over other individuals in micro or everyday contexts. However, it also centralises two things: maintain focus on endemic harms caused by powerful institutions, and recognise the individual impacts these can have on people's lives. Notwithstanding the importance of agency (after all, not everyone knowingly or intentionally inflicts harm, and yet some people do) zemiology aims to highlight ways in which institutional and structural powers connect to micro-level abuses of power which cause harm in the lives of those affected. However, the primary objective should be in documenting, addressing and reducing mass harms which can impact upon people, non-human species and the planet endemically.

be wary of accepting research funds which a) are in the interests of the organisation or institution to be studied and b) require full approval of a governing board before knowledge is disseminated. Moreover, Massoumi *et al.* highlight three key ways in which ethical and professional standards in social scientific research can be compromised: 1) interference with the evidence base (through a lack of transparency on data and conflicts of interest); 2) collaboration on research supporting deception by the state which undermines the ability of citizens to participate in democratic processes; and 3) collaboration on research legitimating human rights abuses, and other coercive state practices (Massoumi *et al.*, 2019: 1). These, and other ways in which critical research can be pre-empted, prevented, distorted and suppressed, are considered at length in the various contributions to Tombs and Whyte's (2003a) edited collection on undertaking research which seeks to hold state and corporate bodies to account. Most fundamentally, however, we need to be clear that the objectives or outcomes of any zemiological project may be in direct contravention of state or corporate priorities and that additional pressures – psychological, physical, legal, institutional – can be placed upon the researcher (Tombs and Whyte, 2003b).

As we can see from Box 5.3, to uncover how harm – in this case, financial harm – is produced and works, we must train our gaze on those who are behind the mechanisms of financial exchange and global banking. From this standpoint, we at least have the potential to deconstruct the workings of social institutions that inflict significant harm. However, as Alex Simpson indicates in the interview, to do so requires the cultural capital to be able to engage with such groups – something which is denied to many due to the very racialised and patriarchal structures that bolster the elite environments within which such social actors reside.

Being creative

We do not intend to outline in any depth what a zemiological methodology looks like, partly because this is not a methods text and there are more than enough versions of those already accessible, but mainly because there is no such thing as zemiological methods. Indeed, as you have seen through the content – and in particular many of the case studies – presented in the chapters to date, all of the main ways of accessing and generating data used across the social sciences are present in zemiological research, from NGO and state-collected statistics, survey data, qualitative materials from oral histories, ethnographies and all forms of interviewing, as well as both critical discourse and content analyses.

Therefore in this final section we wish simply to note that doing zemiology should be creative, innovative – and opportunistic.

As we have noted above, discourse – including imagery – has a key role to play in communicating what harm looks like; and this can be a useful way in generating qualitative data about perceptions and understanding of harms, their impacts, aetiologies, perpetrators, victims, and the relationships between these. The use of imagery – the visual – is central to visual methodologies and there is a likely degree of fit between the panoply of techniques identified by this umbrella term and researching social harm as zemiologists. Gillian Rose has written authoritatively on researching with visual materials

BOX 5.3 RESEARCH CASE STUDY: ALEX SIMPSON ON ACCESSING THE FINANCIAL SERVICE SECTOR IN THE CITY OF LONDON

What was the aim of your study?

The aim of the study was, in short, an examination of social deviance in the City of London. I was not looking at practices that were criminal *per se*, rather I started from the perspective that *finance is harmful* (just look at the 2008 financial crisis). Then, in broadest terms, my unofficial research question was *do these individuals (traders, brokers, investment bankers, etc.) legitimise the harmful practices of their occupational practice?* Borrowing from Matza, it led to an examination of cultural techniques of neutralisation and the cultural reproduction of harm within a powerful industry that, in many ways, sits at the heart of contemporary society.

How did you access the financial service district in the City of London?

The project looked to get an 'up-close' examination of the everyday routines and practices of finance work. Employing an ethnographic methodology, the question of access was one that plagued this project – along with all projects that seek to confront the production of power. I wish I could say that access was sought through a combination of wit and charm, but more prosaically access materialised from cycling.

More a product of accident than design, and following repeated failed attempts to get 'inside' the closed world of the City, members of my cycling club started to hear what I was doing and came forward to be part of the study. Before too long, my strategy was to join club rides across London, often starting at 6am, and talking to people as I went along and tried (more successfully than not) to secure an interview and then ethnographic access. Riding two-by-two along Hertfordshire country lanes, you can begin to think of it as like speed-dating on wheels.

In saying this, cycling is never a methodological strategy. But I view the lesson to be working out the 'sideways' movements we each have into these closed worlds. The culture of cycling overlaps with the culture of the City in many ways (they are both premised on speed, aggression and a masculine ethic of competition) and, as an ad-hoc strategy, it enabled me to get a window into City life.

What barriers did you face in undertaking research/getting interviews?

Again, like nearly all cultural sites of power, there was a strong, protective firewall around the City. This most readily manifested in a culture of silence. My plan of using snowball sampling flatly failed. What manifested was how even one degree of separation was too far. The implicit question that kept on coming back was could they trust me, especially given the potential costs of speaking out. Like most research now, anonymity was a core part of the ethics of conducting interviews, but to give a sense of what these people were thinking, one participant asked me if the transcript could be subpoenaed at all. In honesty, it was not something I had thought of and didn't know. But the fact that it crossed his mind was telling.

The lasting methodological lesson I had from overcoming these challenges is that it is all data. Even when institutions of power use their apparatus of control to keep you out, charting how this works carries meaning. Then when you get small snapshots of the 'inside', how you are controlled, moved and monitored has equal meaning. It may not be what I imagined, but having my retina scanned before being shown into one bank certainly speaks for the amount of security these places operated under… so write it down.

In 50 words … what did you find?

My central finding was the scale of disconnection between the City and the rest of society. This exists in the material construction of the space – kind of an off-shore island moored on the Thames – but also through the attitudes, practices and decisions by people working in the industry.

You can read further on Alex's research in Simpson (2019).

(see, notably, Rose, 2016), and any familiarity with such methods should allow the coherence with the aims, practice and content of zemiology to be readily apparent (see Pauwels and Mannay, 2019).

In his book *A Visual Approach for Green Criminology*, Lorenzo Natali makes original and creative use of visual methods to explore the worlds of those who are the direct victims of various environmental harms. His focus is a town in Southern Spain, Huelva, heavily polluted by local chemical and industrial plants. His approach – photo elicitation – is to use photographs to prompt narratives about experiences and perceptions of the contamination of the town, working with its residents in ways that seek to use these photographs as "a reflexive and collaborative bridge between the subjects and the researchers" (Natali, 2016: iix). Such participatory visual methods cohere entirely with the zemiological project, as does his general argument for the use of flexible methods and concepts which are able to account for the complexity and multi-dimensionality, and therefore the vagueness and elusiveness, of environmental harms. His method is couched within an approach which seeks to rearticulate "the criminological gaze by taking into account, recognizing and including those conflicts, injustices and social harms that would remain excluded by the traditional frames of criminology" thus enhancing the possibility of exposing, confronting, and rendering accountable, the powerful (Natali, 2016: 105).

A particular genre of participative methods are those which are arts-based inquiry and interventions. This covers a broad umbrella of action-based inquiry. Methods within this usually emphasise community based or led approaches and may incorporate drawing, paint-based projects, interactive or drama-based performances or photography.

This set of approaches is an excellent way to engage participants when used appropriately. As well as encouraging groups and communities to work collectively, the outcomes of arts-based inquiry often tell stories in ways that are more accessible for many people, or which can be distributed as part of participant-led strategies. Such practices can also contribute to getting across serious or critical findings in ways which more readily engage non-academics. It is worth nothing however that garnering participation often requires time and effort, and should be done so in ways that are not exploitative or 'pushy' for participants.

Although not necessarily reflective of zemiological inquiry historically, this form of method is incredibly useful for zemiologists who aim to explore harm in more interactive settings, or address harmful experiences in ways that allow participants to lead knowledge development. This way of approaching research is often associated with 'giving voice' to groups that are otherwise often structurally silenced, such as people who are homeless, refugees and asylum-seeking people and so on. This prospect is inherent to the objectives of zemiology – however, we issue caution on assuming that people do not already have voice, since grassroots organisations are often developed and sustained by people affected by harm, or indeed assuming that researchers can truly claim such ability.

It is a truism to state that the method you use is always dependent on what it is you aim to find out. That said, in general, the structural is central to zemiological concerns, but not at the expense of accessing either how dimensions of harm are reproduced at meso – or institutional – levels, and then how these are personally experienced by communities, households, individuals.

As such, developing a mixed methods approach is also useful for uncovering variable dimensions of harm in the context of smaller or localised case study issues. As the example from Chapter 3 highlighted, Canning's research into harms in various Northern European asylum systems used four key methods: critical discourse analysis of relevant media, laws and policies; interviews with people working within British, Danish and Swedish immigration systems such as psychologists, lawyers and immigration detention staff; oral histories with women seeking asylum; and activist ethnographies with asylum support organisations. This facilitated both structural and in-depth insight into otherwise often unseen or silenced harms, such as autonomy harms which develop from the use of everyday controls within asylum centres (Denmark and Sweden) or asylum housing (Britain). Analyses of policy and law show us broad structural patterns; oral histories facilitate insight into the lived realities of demographics affected by political decisions or controls; and interviews with practitioners allow us a glimpse into national and local implications of – in this case, for example – continued welfare and rights restrictions in the lives of people seeking asylum. Moreover, since zemiology has a vested insight in working towards the mitigation or eradication of harmful policy and practice, activist academics such as Canning advocate an active engagement with groups in ways which place positive social change at the fore. This might be done for example in working with organisations and individuals to create practical tools to support the ability of people seeking asylum to understand the whole system, know what potential problems might arise, for example being detained in an Immigration Removal Centre/detention centre, and thus what to do if facing such issues.

Such considerations require us rethinking how we undertake research. As Agozino has recently put it, instead of approaching people from the privileged position of elite scholars, "we should approach the community with the humility that recognizes that data are gifts given to us by willing participants", abandoning the idea of data-collection in favour of "the concept of data-reception". This in turn allows us to eschew the idea that policy recommendations must speak to the state, and embrace the ambition that policy "be reconceptualized as actions that community members themselves could also implement for their self-efficacy". Our role as zemiologists is to prioritise policy actions people can "own and manage themselves even when such actions involve holding state officials more accountable and deepening democracy" (Agozino, 2020: 44).

Finally, we would reiterate that doing zemiology can involve being innovative – especially, to return to our subject of scrutinising the producers of harm, in relation to the powerful, as illustrated in the following focus on Alex Simpson's work on financial services.

Conclusion

As we end this penultimate chapter, there should be clear pathways along which we can now navigate zemiology as a distinct discipline. By all accounts, it sits on the peripheries of various others, not least sociology, critical criminology and critical anthropology, among others, but more fully represents a discipline in its own right.

This chapter in particular advocates a focus on harms of the powerful and of social and cultural elites and institutions, so that we may move more holistically to identifying and addressing larger-scale harms across the social sciences. In doing so, we challenge normative arguments around 'hard to reach' groups, consider ways in which feminist methods and histories such as consciousness raising may be incorporated, and highlight examples of activist engagement and interventions which aim to mitigate harms rather than simply document them. Recognising and reading social research in those terms is for us therefore not simply an echo of Howard Becker's (1967) famous call for a partisan sociology, when he argued for a sociology that declared itself on the side of the powerless underdog. In his response to Becker, Gouldner noted that this perspective had little potential to challenge the social reformist agenda of mainstream sociology. Declaring oneself as 'on the side of the powerless' may have little meaning unless it involves an assault on the powerful: "radical sociologists differ from liberals in that, while they take the standpoint of the underdog, they apply it to the study of the overdogs. Radical sociologists want to study 'power elites'; the leaders or masters of men"[2] (Gouldner, 1970: 51). So doing is one prerequisite for counter-hegemony. This must be the goal of zemiology, and we shall consider this briefly in the final, concluding chapter.

Notes

1 The precise contents of this table are still in development but the main elements are represented here.

2 As with much literature developed by male social scientists, particularly prior to the substantive influence of feminism, we highlight the implications of this gendered term.

References

Agozino, B. (2020) Africana liberation criminologies, in *The Routledge Handbook of Africana Criminologies*, edited by B. Agozino, V. Saleh-Hanna, E. Onyeozili and N. Dastile, Routledge.

Alvesalo-Kuusi, A. and Whyte, D. (2018) Researching the powerful: A call for the reconstruction of research ethics, *Sociological Research Online*, 23 (1), 136–152.

Becker, H. (1967) Whose side are we on? *Social Problems*, 14 (3), 239–247.

Bick, R., Halsey, E. and Ekenga, C. (2018) The global environmental injustice of fast fashion, *Environmental Health*, 92, 1–4.

British Sociological Association (2017) *Statement of Ethical Practice*, www.britsoc.co.uk/media/24310/bsa_statement_of_ethical_practice.pdf

Canning, V. (2017) *Gendered Harm and Structural Violence in the British Asylum System*, Oxon: Routledge.

Canning, V. (2018) Zemiology at the border, in *Zemiology: Reconnecting Crime and Social Harm*, edited by A. Boukli and J. Kotzé, Basingstoke: Palgrave Macmillan, 183–203.

Canning, V. and Matthews, L. (2018), *I'm Just No Good': The Right to Remain Asylum Navigation Board as a Tool for Collective Rights*, Border Criminologies, Oxford University, 20 December, www.law.ox.ac.uk/research-subject-groups/centre-criminology/centreborder-criminologies/blog/2018/12/im-just-no-good (Accessed 16 September 2020).

Cole, M. (2020) Criminology, harm and non-human animals, in *Crime, Harm and the State. Book 1*, edited by L. Copson, E. Dimou and S. Tombs, Milton Keynes: Open University Press, 111–143.

DeMartino, G. (2019) Econogenic harm and the case for 'Economy Harm Profile' analysis, *New Political Economy*, 24 (6), 798–815.

Du Bois, W. E. B. (1898) The Study of the Negro Problems, *The Annals of the American Academy of Political and Social Science*, January, 1–23.

Emejulu, A. and Sobande, F. (2019) *To Exist Is to Resist – Black Feminism in Europe*, London: Pluto Press.

Foucault, M. (1972) *The Archaeology of Knowledge*, London: Pantheon Books.

Foucault, M. (1977) *Discipline and Punish*, London: Allen Lane.

Gouldner, A. W. (1970) *The Coming Crisis of Western Sociology*, London: Heinemann.

Karlsen, S., Carver, N., Mogilnicka, M. and Pantazis, C. (2019) *"Stigmatising" and "Traumatising" Approaches to FGM Need Urgent Review*. Policy Report 49, March, University of Bristol, file:///D:/Articles/Routledge%20book/Policy%20Report%2046%20Feb%2019%20FGM%20Safeguarding.pdf (Accessed 22 June 2020).

Klaas, P., Berge, K., Klaas, K., Klaas, J. and Larson, A. (2014) When patients are harmed, but are not wronged: Ethics, law, and history, *Mayo Clin Proc.*, 89 (9), 1279–1286.

Large, J. (2018) Spot the fashion victim(s): The importance of rethinking harm within the context of fashion counterfeiting, in *Zemiology: Reconnecting Crime and Social Harm*, edited by A. Boukli and J. Kotzé, Basingstoke: Palgrave Macmillan, 223–245.

Lloyd, A. (2018) *The Harms of Work*, Bristol: Policy Press.

Malloch, M. (2016) Justice for women: A penal utopia?, *Justice, Power and Resistance: Foundation Issue: Non-penal Real Utopias*, 1 (1), 151–169.

Massoumi, N., Mills, T. and Miller, D. (2019) Secrecy, coercion and deception in research on 'terrorism' and 'extremism', *Contemporary Social Science*, online first: http://hdl.handle.net/10871/37167 (Accessed 14 January 2020).

Mathiesen, T. and Hjemdal, O. K. (2016) A new look at victim and offender: An abolitionist approach, *Justice, Power and Resistance: Foundation Issue: Non-penal Real Utopias*, 1 (1), 137–150.

Natali, L. (2016) *A Visual Approach for Green Criminology*, Basingstoke: Palgrave.

Patel, T. and Tyrer, D. (2011) *Race, Crime and Resistance*, London: Sage.

Pauwels, L. and Mannay, D., eds. (2019) *The SAGE Handbook of Visual Research Methods*, 2nd ed., London: Sage.

Prison Reform Trust (2019) *Bromley Briefings Prison Factfile, Winter 2019*, www.prisonreformtrust.org.uk/Portals/0/Documents/Bromley%20Briefings/Winter%202019%20Factfile%20web.pdf (Accessed 10 June 2020).

Rose, G. (2016) *Visual Methodologies: An Introduction to Researching with Visual Materials*, 4th ed., London: Sage.

Schelhase, M. (2020) Bringing the harm home: The quest for home ownership and the amplification of social harm, *New Political Economy*, DOI: 10.1080/13563467.2020.1782363

Simončič, K. (2017) Addressing the collateral damage of fast fashion: The perception of social harm and the possibility of consumer agency, in *Emerging Voices: Critical Social Research by European Group Early Career and Postgraduate Researchers*, edited by S. Fletcher and H. Whyte, Weston-super-Mare: EG Press, 203–214.

Simpson, Alex (2019) The culture of moral disengagement and harm production in the City of London's financial services industry, *Justice, Power and Resistance*, 3 (1), 115–133.

Soliman, F. (2019) States of exception, human rights and social harm: Towards a border zemiology, *Theoretical Criminology*, online first: 1–19.

Tombs, S. and Whyte, D., eds. (2003a) *Unmasking the Crimes of the Powerful: Scrutinising States and Corporations*, New York/London: Peter Lang.

Tombs, S. and Whyte, D. (2003b) Researching the powerful: Contemporary political economy and critical social science, in *Unmasking the Crimes of the Powerful: Scrutinising States and Corporations*, edited by S. Tombs and D. Whyte, New York/London: Peter Lang, 3–45.

Tombs, S. and Whyte, D. (2017) Worker safety, in *Oxford Research Encyclopedia of Criminology and Criminal Justice*, edited by H. Pontell, New York: Oxford University Press, https://oxfordre.com/criminology/view/10.1093/acrefore/9780190264079.001.0001/acrefore-9780190264079-e-270?rskey=0nnUM8&result=1

Walters, R. (2018) Climate change denial: Making ignorance great again, in *Ignorance, Power and Harm: Agnotology and the Criminological Imagination*, edited by A. Barton and H. Davis, Basingstoke: Palgrave Macmillan, 163–187.

White, R. (2018) *Climate Change Criminology*, Bristol: Bristol University Press.

CONCLUSION

Activist zemiology for social justice

Introduction

We began this book by locating the emergence of social harm at the margins of criminology – in critical criminologies – at the end of the last century. We then traced the variants of a social harm perspectives, teasing out their relationships to critical criminologies – where it became clear, for us, 20 years into work around social harm, that we were no longer discussing a 'New Direction in Critical Criminology', as the title of this book series might suggest, but a departure from, a clear shift *beyond*, criminology: towards a new discipline, zemiology.

In seeking to mark out the nature, commitments and parameters of that discipline we have sought to clarify the concept of social harm which is at its centre – its dimensions, its dynamic forms and its essential elements, via both a provisional typology and an ontology of harm. We then considered some of the methodological principles of zemiological investigation. It goes without saying that all of this work is unfinished, perhaps necessarily so. As Goyes has argued, "To adopt a harm perspective is to accept that it is impossible to enumerate exhaustively all the situations that impair the health of humans, non-humans and the eco-system" (Goyes, 2019: 514).

But the corollary of this latter observation is that zemiology is rich with possibility. Zemiology may develop in some predictable ways – such as further understanding the ways in which socio-economic organisations of various societies increase harms such as child poverty, as discussed earlier in the book (Pemberton, 2015). But equally, bottom-up zemiology will uncover previously un-named harms, such as the gendered impacts of autonomy harms addressed in Canning's research with women seeking asylum (Canning, 2019a, 2019b), or the violence of 'stuckedness' to which we referred in Chapter 4, following Iliadou (2019).

So there is enormous scope for the development of zemiology, that is empirically, conceptually, methodologically – and politically. In other words, zemiology is not simply about revealing harm as a result of state, corporate or pro-capitalist, racialised, gendered practices, processes, institutions and sentiments – its objective in exposing is challenging and eradicating harm and thereby furthering social justice. If criminology began its life in the service of the state, zemiology has emerged as a disciplinary focus committed to challenging state power, and those agents and institutions which bolster and are supported by that power. From this commitment, a key corollary is that zemiology must be a participative and co-operative activity, operating beyond academic borders – zemiology, we would argue, only makes sense as an activist as well as an academic activity.

Rejecting the myth of value freedom

We have long argued – albeit hardly uniquely – that the myths of value freedom and value neutrality in criminological and indeed social scientific research need to be abandoned (Canning, 2017, 2018; Hillyard *et al.*, 2004; Tombs, 2015; Tombs and Whyte, 2003a, 2003b, 2020). They are not only false illusions, but they serve to maintain power, to limit imagination and to restrict possibilities for effective social change – which, we shall argue, must be the goal of zemiological research.

In the context of this statement regarding the illusions of value freedom and value neutrality, let us make several observations.

First, the *absence* of 'value-neutrality' is a feature of all forms of research, despite the fact that this is rarely acknowledged by those who conduct more mainstream and, for example, state or corporate funded research. Although this is discussed extensively as a problem in, for example, the literature on ethnography, where it is often described as 'going native' (see, for example, Punch, 1993), accusations of *bias* or *subjectivity* are rare where organisations have granted access on their own terms or even funded research. On the contrary, such associations, especially when it comes to large corporations and government departments, are often worn as badges of honour, or credibility (McClung, 1978), and at the same time reinforce the pretensions of the badge wearer to be the guardians of more robust and even more 'objective' knowledge.

Second, to reject value-neutrality is not to deny that there are implications of viewing the world from a particular perspective. But such problems – always highlighted by those with pretensions to value-neutrality and commitments to liberal virtue of 'balance' (Jackson, 2011) – are at least mitigated where researchers recognise, describe and are open about the perspective from which their research commitments, questions and modes of analysis and dissemination originate. Put simply, we can only start to value objectivity in social research after we recognise that much of the research conducted in western liberal democracies – particularly that which relies upon the consent or support of large organisations – is highly partisan in the first place (Pearce, 1993). The historical development of the social sciences has been inseparable from 'partisanship', never 'value-neutral'. So questioning whether partisanship is desirable or not makes little sense since social scientists, by definition, *are* partisan (Hobsbawm, 1998: 179–180).

Third, then, to eschew value-freedom does not deny openness, accountability, rigour, honesty and transparency, and indeed for some nor does it mean that we cannot retain reference to objectivity (Agozino, 2020). But following our previous points, these requirements should apply to *all* researchers. All research is value laden, and if there are value commitments which underpin any piece of research then there are, therefore, implicitly or explicitly, particular interests which it might further (and might not). These are choices which all researchers make, whether they recognise them or not. As Gramsci (1971) argued, the romantic ideal of the 'ivory tower' – where research is conducted which is neutral, value-free and divorced from the partisan imperatives of economic, political and social forces – has always been a highly fetishised but very powerful one for those intellectuals who see themselves as non-aligned. But it is as value laden a choice as a statement that one is engaged in work to pursue class, gender or racial justice.

Fourth, none of these observations apply with greater or lesser force to any particular method or data. Thus, it is now widely accepted across social sciences that data does not speak for itself, that there is no greater neutrality in quantitative over qualitative data, that all data represents the values and choices made by those collecting the data – whether this be Ministry of Justice crime statistics or oral histories of exploitation and suffering. At the same time, there are a range of processes which inflect and infect the practice of knowledge production and knowledge claims. These latter are well documented, and range from the perceived status of the researchers (and their institutional affiliations), the availability of funding for research, the ability to gain access to data, and a variety of barriers to dissemination, including no-platforming, confidentiality, slander and libel laws. Some of these aspects of this dimension of the myth of objectivity are illustrated via a social phenomenon to which we are all often alerted to: terrorism, as you can see in Box C.1.

BOX C.1 TERRORISM RESEARCH AND PREVENTION STRATEGIES AS A CASE STUDY

As you are likely to be aware, in the aftermath of the 9/11 attacks in the United States, many nations across the globe prioritised research and terror prevention strategies, including in the United Kingdom. Where previously terrorism in the UK had been narrowly associated with militant Irish Republicanism (and to a lesser extent Northern Irish Loyalism), the stereotype of a 'terrorist' became associated with typified Muslims and people from Middle Eastern heritage. As various other violent attacks were perpetrated in London and Paris, amongst others globally, the focus on this form of terrorism intensified almost overnight.

However, although clearly severely harmful, the social reality has remained that terrorism of this kind contributes to very few deaths in the UK. Between April 2003 and March 2019, 92 terror-related deaths were recorded. In fact, the two clear peaks of terror-related deaths were not in England, but in Northern Ireland (344 during the conflict in 1972) and Scotland (271 as a result of the Lockerbie bombing in 1988) (see Allen and Kirk-Wade, 2020). As a compass, statistical estimates from Steve Tombs suggest that anywhere between 13,000 and 50,000 people die in work *each year* in the UK (2014), whilst statistics show that 149 women were killed in the UK by 147 men in 2018 alone (Femicide Consensus, 2020). However, funding for research and interventions is outweighed by the state focus on terrorism, even though it is much less likely to contribute to deaths of the general population. In 2015, for example, a year which registered zero terror-related deaths, the then Chancellor of the Exchequer George Osbourne pledged £15.1 billion to counterterrorism efforts (Barber, 2015).

As well as demonstrating that a holistic approach to statistical analysis can be incredibly helpful to zemiological studies, this also reminds us that what we consider to be of grave significance to societies is often driven by state-based agendas rather than simply what is empirically most harmful for us. As interrogative research by Massoumi *et al.* (2019) evidence, these agendas create environments which are far from objective – indeed the opposite is true. Their use of Freedom of Information Requests, combined with rigorous participation in the development of terrorism research centres, showed that secret research laboratories as well as university-based research centres were directly or indirectly funded by the British state. In one centre, the Centre for Research and Evidence on Security Threat based at the University of Lancaster, this was presented under a call from a public body, the Economic and Social Research Council. On closer inspection, the funds were distributed directly by the 'UK security and intelligence agencies'.

As we scratch the surface then, it becomes clear that the prospect of fully objective research of any form is not possible in the social sciences as some academics would like to present. This is important: using the work of Massoumi *et al.* as a case study, we are able to see that research can actually determine what we come to 'know' or prioritise as harm in society. And yet as they evidence in this example, the employing of the Official Secrets Act (which is otherwise uncommon for researchers to have to adhere to in a democracy) as well as non-disclosures of who has funded the research, coupled with forced redactions of findings, serves to remind us that claims of research objectivity and transparency require rigorous examination.

Choosing activist zemiology

As we have argued, following others, knowledge for social justice must eschew the myth of value freedom and be committed to achieving social justice through progressive social change. In the words of Biko Agozino, "Racist-imperialist-patriarchal oppression is real" and must be studied with "the commitment to end it". So we cannot engage in "critical thinking without the dual emphasis on activism. Let us talk the talk and walk the walk in opposition to all systems of oppression and in favor of liberation" (Agozino, 2020: 43).

In fact, we have both always considered our academic work to have been and be a form of political activism, a claim and a phrase upon which we'd like to make several observations.

The first thing to say is to echo that alluded to above – which is in one sense to deny the distinction between activists and academics. For this distinction, or dichotomy, is an association, implicit or otherwise, between academics and the 'ivory tower', activists and the real world, distinctions which are, ironically, highly ideological and support claims on the part of the academy to be producing disinterested, value-free knowledge – usually entirely supportive of the status quo.

Second, then, and following from the previous point, we have both made very explicit choices about engaging in politicised research. And we have encountered criticisms for that choice and that activity at times. But as we have said, all of us have a choice to make, whether we make that explicit or even whether we recognise it. All academics can choose what they claim or believe to be disengaged, disinterested 'value-free' research – but this in itself is as political a choice as that which we and many others have made to engage in explicitly politicised work.

Third, being active involves a wide variety of activities. These include writing – by which we mean books, journal articles, book chapters, pamphlets, leaflets and flyers, blogs, letters to newspapers, writing and contributing to position papers, organisational and Party manifestos, written evidence to Select Committees and to formal consultation processes. Note that many or most of these are not considered in the plethora of league tables universities are subject to, and it is certainly the case that pressures on newer academics become ever more intense in the era of the neo-liberal university – so more established academic colleagues need to provide support, space and resources to allow others to engage in such work. Beyond writing, we've been fortunate enough to be involved in making podcasts, radio programmes, documentaries, as well as TV and radio. We've spoken at Union and political conferences, as well as at demonstrations and assemblies, large and (usually!) small in high streets, at docks and outside factory gates, and in Parliaments. We have been on demonstrations, occupations, sit-ins, walk-outs and vigils. Most of all, being active has involved developing long-term relationships of trust and reciprocity – one aspect of which is to organise events including workshops, debates, conferences, seminars, and so on.

Lastly, it has been our pleasure to do so, and to our benefit. We have each met lots of fantastic people, made lifelong friends, been to places and spaces we otherwise would not have visited, and had access to data and insights we would otherwise never have encountered. So our work with counter-hegemonic organisations has not been borne out of altruism. Far from it. At the same time, we do recognise, as perhaps we all must, that however we are employed as academics, academic work is relatively privileged. It is relatively well-paid, and importantly it carries status. These privileges are highly differentially distributed, and less so as universities move further toward neo-liberalisation. One of us, as a white, late-middle-aged male professor, is at the apex of such privilege; the other, a younger, mid-career woman academic, albeit in a secure permanent post, is less so. So the obligation and the opportunity that we all have to 'give back' is, too, differentially distributed. None of this, of course, is to obscure some of the complexities of undertaking academic activism – as Deanna Dadusc, an academic and activist working on the rights of migrants crossing the Mediterranean, tells us (Box C.2).

Moreover, if we have both been activist in our work, we would also argue that we have both been zemiological – even before zemiology! That is, we

BOX C.2 INTERVIEW WITH DEANNA DADUSC

What are the difficulties in juggling academia and activism?

Here I would say that the combination of academic burn-out + activism burn-out is the main difficulty of juggling these two draining worlds, but maybe I would like to start with something broader on the relation between academia and activism.

Academia and activism sometimes feel as worlds apart, while at times they seem inseparable, to the extent that theory and practice cannot be separated. Activism does not need academic theorising and critique, as activists are producing in-depth analysis of the relations of power they are struggling against. However, academia needs to learn from ongoing struggles in order to fully understand the impact and the mechanisms of state and corporate harms.

Especially when discussing state and corporate harms, for me it has been impossible to conduct research without being actively involved in political struggles that were fighting against these issues and standing in solidarity with the people directly affected. It is only through these everyday experiences that I could learn the techniques of criminalisation of activism by the state, as well as how state-corporate violence and harm are constantly protected by the law.

What are the biggest issues you face in undertaking research along activism?

The main difficulty is how to conduct academic research without appropriating or 'stealing' the collective knowledge produced by activists. In activist struggle there is often a suspicion towards academic knowledge production, and especially towards researchers that turn social movements into objects of study, exploiting activist experiences and appropriating collective voices for individual academic publications.

Conducting activist-research for me it is not about 'observing social movements' but elaborating critiques and analysis from the perspective of active resistance to harm and structural violence. The questions we need to ask, are not so much 'how are movements organised?', but 'how can we learn from these experiences and produce knowledge that can contribute to social justice?'.

It is also important to avoid the creation of hierarchies between activist practice and academic theorising. As activist-academics, we cannot contribute to social justice only by writing and theorising. In my involvement in horizontal, self-organised struggles it has always been crucial to share all roles and tasks – from taking night shifts for the Alarm Phone, to cooking, cleaning and building barricades in the (criminalised) occupied spaces I lived in.

What do you think universities could do to support research and activism relating to harm?

Time, of course. But also space and resources. Neo-liberal academia offers little space for activist engagement, as well as for activists to participate into academic spaces.

Besides resources, the main obstacle that needs to be overcome is the way knowledge production and research is valued, funded and supported. Activist knowledge is often dismissed as biased, not objective. While feminist, decolonial and militant researchers acknowledge the impossibility of 'value-free' or 'objective' knowledge production, there is still a strong belief that researchers need to be detached from politics.

have worked across disciplines – our backgrounds and 'training' span economics, political economy, political theory, and sociology. We have both focused upon harms at the margins of or entirely outwith definitions of crime and criminal justice systems. And we have both, as indicated above, sought to further social justice not as an adjunct to but as a central motivation of our work.

Moreover, as zemiologists engaged in both empirical research and activism, we have sought to ensure working closely with grassroot institutions or NGOs over long, sustained periods of time. We emphasise that this is not to advocate activist engagement *as a means to access groups*, which in itself is exploitative and harmful, but rather vice versa: our long-term involvement with such groups and the issues around which they struggle has prompted zemiological research with a sustained focus on various forms of harm. In some instances, such engagement can also mean exploring harmful dynamics within non-governmental organisations and campaign groups since, even with the best intentions, these are far from being exempt from creating or sustaining harmful practices. Thus, for example, Downes (2017) addresses sexual violence in Left movements in the UK, while Richey and Ponte (2011) critically examine the commodification of aid and finance amongst charities, not least those working globally with 'celebrities'. Indeed, this is a tricky area since those working against harmful structures such as patriarchy, heterosexism and racism are easily undermined by dominant institutions or political parties who inflict the same harms, but represent these aspects as failures of counter-hegemonic groups. As such there can be a tendency to 'hush up' harmful actors or actions when the overall objective is for the greater good, but harm requires deconstruction and dismantlement wherever possible.

Doing zemiology, then, is to accept that it is to recognise that:

> an activist stance in which perceptions of victimized individuals are taken as valid knowledge is the only way to coherently implement a harm perspective, where what is considered a problem is not imposed by researchers but dialectically built with the prominent participation of the victims.
>
> *(Goyes, 2019: 514)*

This requires action to actively support harm mitigation.

In any case, where working with social groups is concerned, we advocate embedding grassroots approaches, including co-production of knowledge in undertaking or disseminating research from organisation-led objectives and agendas. Whilst this may not necessarily appear a requisite of desk-based research, the inclusion of groups affected by or experiencing potentially harmful environments should be engaged with, so that priorities remain community based, rather than solely in academic knowledge attainment. A dual, two-way process is therefore encouraged to ensure ethically founded research relationships which work toward offering back to communities and organisations rather than solely producing or reproducing knowledge which becomes confined to academia.

Given that zemiology is focused on developing conceptual and empirical evidence around harms, violence may be a central facet of some studies or analyses. Since violence – in particular sexualised, domestic or interpersonal violence – has a unique history of social silencing through shame and stigmatisation, it is important that prevalence, experience and impacts of violence are exposed. There is also cause for concern that by labelling survivors of violence as inherently vulnerable, particularly when institutions decide instead to avoid research based on the above issues, then there develops a secondary silencing. So whilst it is important that harms, in this case the outcomes of abuses or physical or sexualised violence, are centralised in zemiological research, and given the possibility of negative impacts, we advocate points raised by Downes *et al.* who put forward the following:

> recommendations for ethical decision-making in violence and abuse research: (i) to reconsider participants as active agents and stakeholders; (ii) to prioritise the development of skilled researchers; (iii) to develop situated processes of informed consent and confidentiality; and (iv) to continue to discuss and share practical experiences of feminist research practice that seeks to deliver justice and social change.
>
> *(Downes et al., 2014)*

Zemiology, social harm, social justice

The final, key, but perhaps most obvious point to make here – and one on which it is fitting to conclude – is in fact to return to an observation made in *Beyond Criminology*: namely, that a zemiological focus inevitably and conclusively leads us away from identifying responses to social problems which are located in or around the criminal justice system. And this, too, must be our aim as activists, recognising that criminal justice processes are mechanisms of pain delivery – that is, they are sites and forms of harmful practices in themselves, a point which is now so well-documented even in critical criminology that it hardly bears reiterating. Thus, in keeping with abolitionist perspectives, an activist zemiology recognises that criminal justice is inherently linked to state, class, gendered and racialised power and is never part of a progressive struggle for greater social justice even where it seems to offer quick fixes. Thus a defining feature of the zemiological enterprise must be to identify alternative forms of harm response and mitigation in ways which are coherent with the good society, a post-capitalism where social harms – those assumptions, practices, policies, processes and social arrangements which deny or inhibit the flourishing of what it is to be human – are minimised if not absent.

This demand to seek alternative responses to social problems might at first appear to be highly challenging – but on closer inspection the problems it poses are less about identifying alternative policy responses to social harm, but in overcoming the political obstacles to implementing them. So we would argue, for example, there is now clear evidence that corporate harm is less amenable to legal reform due to the essentially destructive nature of the corporate form – so that corporate structures at worst need disruption (Tombs, 2016) via redistributions of power or at best dismantling so that the corporation must be abolished (Tombs and Whyte, 2015; Whyte, 2020). Or, questions of street crime or the propensity to re-commit after being processed through the criminal justice system – 'recidivism' – almost by definition evade criminal justice solutions; rather, they are matters for mental and public health services, employment and training, housing and empathetic and well-funded social and welfare services.

Further, let us be clear that zemiology requires us to be imaginative, idealistic, utopian and pragmatic. Thus, being opposed to being reformist does not mean eschewing reforms.

The first thing we have to do is reject the idea that being idealistic can never be pragmatic or useful in winning concessions or influencing policy. But it depends what these reforms are, what they achieve – and what they pre-empt. Many critical criminologists – who will be reading this book as a part of a Critical Criminology Series – recognise the harms of various state or corporate functions, such as the harms of imprisonment, and work to reform conditions. This is important: for example, people confined in prisons may benefit from improved access to books, better food or living conditions; engaging in rehabilitative therapies may also help some individuals emotionally and psychologically. However, zemiologists would point to the structural make-up of prison populations – that those confined are almost exclusively poor, disproportionately Black, with high levels of people entering with mental health problems or learning disabilities. This indicates that the structures in society working to control poorer populations – again embedded in historically elitist definitions of 'crime' – may be the key contributor to the problems here.

Second, and following this, a reformist discourse and agenda can, under some circumstances, bolster more radical movements for fundamental social change. Thus, it is possible to remain outside the ideological terrain of the state and at the same time to engage on the terrain of the policy world or with the current political system. In fact, there are a number of counter-hegemonic groups that stand firmly and unapologetically in opposition to the state's regulatory agenda but still remain engaged with government in consultations, lobbying and policy work. Those groups, such as the Hazards Campaign and its network of Hazards centres, I or NQUEST, have shown us that idealism does not necessarily constrain the effectiveness or political impact of counter-hegemonic struggle. Therefore, the question remains: how best we might develop a pragmatic idealism that revolves around making connections between, and interventions across, state, economy, politics, history and 'culture', and which stands in direct opposition to 'principled pluralism' with its 'tendencies towards fragmentary problems and scattered causation' (Mills, 1970: 104). Or, as Rosa Luxembourg put it in relation to social democracy and reformative action, "The struggle for reforms is its means, the social revolution, its goal" (1899/1990: 369).

For us, avoiding these tendencies is dependent upon us retaining an element of utopianism – our demands and our actions must be achievable yet at the same time unashamedly utopian (Wright, 2015), and this is intrinsic to the zemiological enterprise. And, following Jacoby, we would argue that these should be utopian in an 'iconoclastic' rather than 'blueprint' sense (Jacoby, 2005). Further, not least if we are to avoid political immobilisation likely to be induced by a perceived need to set out a blueprint which lays down an image of a future utopia in detail, we should, as one commentator has put it, "learn to think about capitalism coming to an end without assuming responsibility for answering the question of what one proposes to put in its place" (Streeck, 2014: 46).

Thinking and achieving social justice will not be done through the criminal justice system nor the state nor through its constituent institutions. It will not be done by academics called zemiologists, nor will it be done by 'them', some unspecified activists 'out there', beyond academia. It will be a collective, participatory imaginative enterprise. Zemiology, however, can at least be a part of the solution rather than a part of the problem – an academic activity where it is not just possible but necessary to be part of the struggle for social justice.

References

Agozino, B. (2020) Africana liberation criminologies, in *The Routledge Handbook of Africana Criminologies*, edited by B. Agozino, V. Saleh-Hanna, E. Onyeozili and N. Dastile.

Allen, G. and Kirk-Wade, E. (2020) *Terrorism in Great Britain: The Statistics*, London: House of Commons, file:///C:/Users/Vicky/Downloads/CBP-7613.pdf (Accessed 15 December 2020(,

Barber, L. (2015) Autumn Statement 2015: George Osborne promises £3.4bn extra counter-terrorism spending in wake of Paris attacks but no police cuts commitment, *City AM*, www.cityam.com/autumn-statement-and-comprehensive-spending-review-2015-george-osborne-promises-30pc-increase-in-counter-terrorism-spending-in-wake-of-paris-attacks/ (Accessed 7 July 2020.

Canning, V. (2017) *Gendered Harm and Structural Violence in the British Asylum System*, Oxon: Routledge.

Canning, V. (2018) Zemiology at the border, in *Zemiology: Reconnecting Crime and Social Harm*, edited by A. Boukli and J. Kotzé, Basingstoke: Palgrave Macmillan, 183–203.

Canning, V. (2019a) *Reimagining Refugee Rights: Addressing Asylum Harms in Britain, Denmark and Sweden*, Migration and Mobilities Bristol, www.statewatch.org/news/2019/mar/uk-dk-se-reimagining-refugee-rights-asylum-harms-3–19.pdf (Accessed 15 December 2020).

Canning, V. (2019b) Degradation by design: Women seeking asylum in Northern Europe, *Race & Class*, July.

Downes, J. (2017) 'It's not the abuse that kills you, it's the silence': The silencing of sexual violence activism in social justice movements in the UK Left, *Justice, Power and Resistance*, 1 (2), 35–58.

Downes, J., Kelly, L. and Westmarland, N. (2014) Ethics in violence and abuse research – a positive empowerment approach, *Sociological Research Online*, 19 (1), 29–41.

Femicide Census (2020) *Femicide Census 2018*, https://femicidescensus.org/reports/ (Accessed 7 July 2020).

Goyes, D. R. (2019) *A Southern Green Criminology: Science against Ecological Discrimination*, Bingley: Emerald.

Gramsci, A. (1971) *Selections from the Prison Notebooks of Antonio Gramsci*, edited and translated by Q. Hoare and G. Nowell Smith, London: Lawrence and Wishart.

Hillyard, P. and Tombs, S. (2004) Beyond criminology?, in *Beyond Criminology: Taking Harm Seriously*, edited by P. Hillyard, C. Pantazis, S. Tombs and D. Gordon, London: Pluto Press, 10–29.

Hobsbawm, E. (1998) *On History*, London: Abacus.

Iliadou, E. (2019) *Border Harms and Everyday Violence: The Lived Experiences of Border Crossers in Lesvos Island, Greece*, PhD Thesis in Criminology and Social Policy, Open University, January.

Jackson, W. (2011) Liberal intellectuals and the politics of security, in *Anti-Security*, edited by M. Neocleous and G. Rigakos, Ottawa: Red Quill Books, 165–189.

Jacoby, R. (2005) *Picture Imperfect: Utopian Thought for an Anti-Utopian Age*, New York: Columbia University Press.

Luxemburg, R. (1899/1990) Sozialreform oder Revolution [Social Reform or Revolution?], *Leipziger Volkszeitung*, in Rosa Luxemburg, *Gesammelte Werke [Collected Works], Vol. 1, 1893–1905*, Berlin: Dietz, 369–371.

Massoumi, N., Mills, T. and Miller, D. (2019) Secrecy, coercion and deception in research on 'terrorism' and 'extremism', *Contemporary Social Science*, online first: http://hdl.handle.net/10871/37167 (Accessed 14 January 2020).

McClung, L. (1978) *Sociology for Whom?* New York: Oxford University Press.

Mills, C.W. (1970) *The Sociological Imagination*, London: Penguin.

Pearce, F. (1993) Corporate rationality as corporate crime, *Studies in Political Economy*, 40, 135–162.

Pemberton, S. (2015) *Harmful Societies: Understanding Social Harm*, Bristol: Policy Press.

Punch, M. (1993) Observation and the Police: The research experience, in *Social Research: Philosophy, Politics and Practice*, edited by M. Hammersley, London: Sage, 181–199.

Richey, L. A. and Ponte, S. (2011) *Brand Aid: Shopping Well to Save the World*, USA: Minnesota University Press.

Streeck, W. (2014) How will capitalism end?, *New Left Review*, 87, 35–64.

Tombs, S. (2014) Hard evidence: Are work-related deaths in decline?, *The Conversation*, 29 October, https://theconversation.com/hard-evidence-are-work-related-deaths-in-decline-33553 (Accessed 7 July 2020).

Tombs, S. (2015) Crisis, what crisis? Regulation and the academic orthodoxy, *Special Issue of The Howard Journal of Criminal Justice*, 54 (1), 57–72.
Tombs, S. (2016) What to do with the harmful corporation?, *Justice, Power and Resistance*, 1 (1), 193–216.
Tombs, S. and Whyte, D., eds. (2003a) *Unmasking the Crimes of the Powerful: Scrutinising States and Corporations*, New York/London: Peter Lang.
Tombs, S. and Whyte, D. (2003b) Researching the powerful: Contemporary political economy and critical social science, in *Unmasking the Crimes of the Powerful: Scrutinising States and Corporations*, edited by S. Tombs and D. Whyte, 3–45.
Tombs, S. and Whyte, D. (2015) *The Corporate Criminal: Why Corporations Must Be Abolished*, Oxon: Routledge.
Tombs, S. and Whyte, D. (2020) Struggles inside and outside the university, in *Resisting the Punitive State*, edited by J. Greener, E. Hart and R. Moth, London: Pluto, 46–67.
Whyte, D. (2020) *Ecocide: Kill the Corporation before It Kills Us*, Manchester: Manchester University Press.
Wright, O. (2015) Paris attacks: Women targeted as hate crime against British Muslims soars following terrorist atrocity, *The Independent*, 22 November, www.independent.co.uk/news/uk/home-news/paris-attacks-british-muslims-face-300-spike-in-racial-attacks-in-week-following-terror-a6744376.html (Accessed 19 June 2020).

INDEX

Note: Page numbers in *italics* indicate figures and in **bold** indicate tables on the corresponding pages.